GOOD THINGS FROM
TAG SALES
and
flea markets

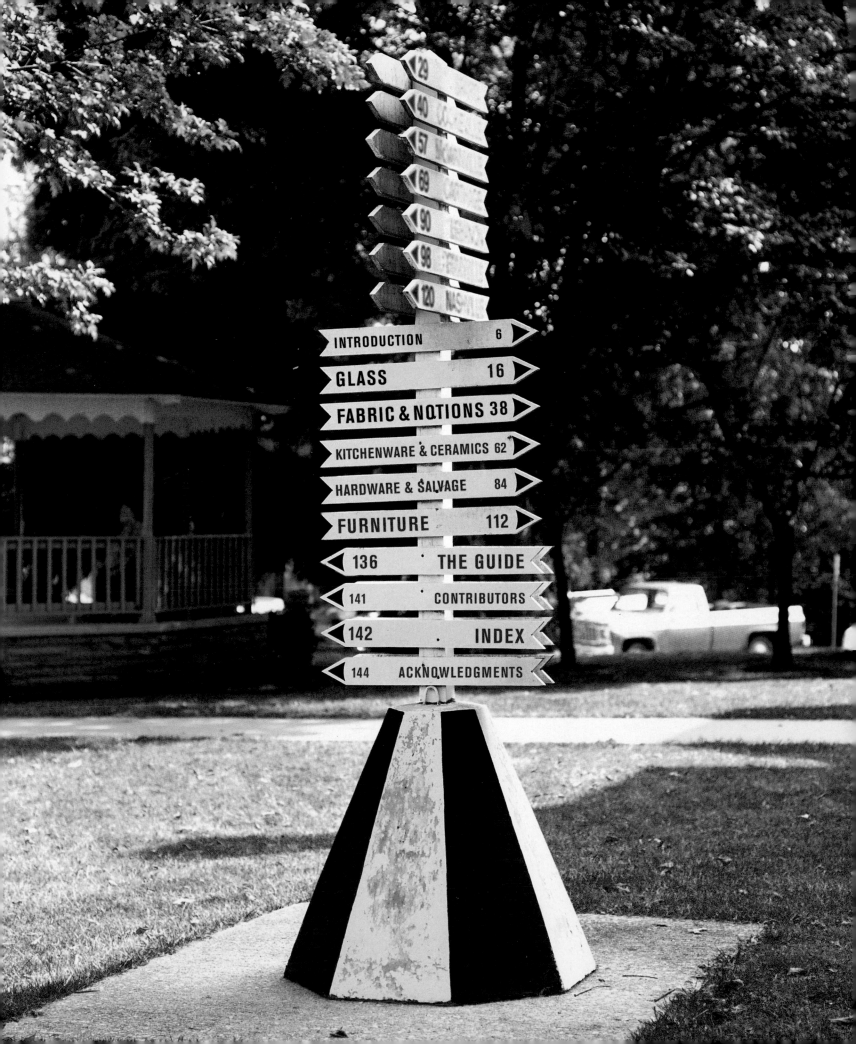

EVERYONE LOVES A TAG SALE OR FLEA MARKET, WHERE TEMPT-
ING VINTAGE GOODS LIE IN NEAT PILES, SCATTERED DISPLAYS,

or messy mounds, just waiting to be rediscovered. You never know what you might find or how little you will have to pay for it. Many shoppers look at these opportunities as ways to meet specific collecting goals (completing that chintzware tea service, for example, or adding to a closetful of Victorian petticoats), but it pays to have a broader view. Shopping a flea market or tag sale can be an exercise in creative foraging. It is a chance to discover wonderful, inexpensive objects that, with a little help, can lead new lives in wholly different guises. Whether it's a Bakelite belt buckle that lives on as a miniature picture frame or an old damask bedspread that upholsters an ottoman in sumptuous style, a vintage treasure can present endless possibilities. The

challenge is to see beyond an item's original purpose, visualizing instead the ways in which it can work for you now. Objects that were manufactured before the throwaway era of polyester and plastic usually combine high-quality materials with good design—and are often sold at basement prices. The fine linen of an embroidered handkerchief, the heavy enamel of an old electrical fixture, and the geometric pattern of a dessert mold still catch and hold the eye. That these items have fallen out of common use need not deter you. There are other options: Stretch and frame the handkerchief; turn the fixture into a sleek candleholder for a dining table; hang an artful arrangement of dessert and salad molds on your kitchen wall. When you see a pleasing form, take a few moments to let your imagination suggest a new function. Don't pass up a funky wrought-iron plant stand because it is old and rusty or you lack a green thumb. With one can of butter-yellow paint you can turn it into a charming bookshelf for a child's bedroom.

Damaged finds present other opportunities: A chair with a broken back may work as a stool; a handleless teacup may serve as the base of a china compote. A weathered surface can be either appreciated as is or easily spruced up: Celebrate the patina on a garden urn by bringing it inside and using it to hold logs beside your fireplace; paint a worn enamel stepladder a clean, glossy white before loading it with fluffy towels in the guest bathroom. Other problems with the condition of a find can inspire you: Look past the holes in a $5 damask tablecloth to its perfectly preserved center medallion. You can cut out this intricate design and make it the face of a one-of-a-kind throw pillow.

Anyone can easily learn how to spot the hidden purpose in a flea-market find. In these pages we share our best hunting-and-gathering tips and techniques for vintage-shopping sites, and provide dozens of clever suggestions for coaxing inexpensive, readily available odds and ends into rich new roles.

WHAT IS A TAG SALE AND HOW CAN YOU FIND ONE?

The tag sale (also known as a garage sale or yard sale) is a twentieth-century innovation generated by the modern desire to eliminate clutter. These sales take their name from the price tags placed on every item. Tag sales are organized not by dealers but by families or individuals who put things they no longer want or need on their lawns or in their garages, and offer them for sale. Some sales are single-home affairs, but often neighbors will band together and pool their unwanted belongings to attract more buyers. Tag sales are almost always held on weekends in the late spring, summer, or early fall, most often in suburban or thickly settled rural areas. Among the usual pickings are toys, books, kitchen equipment, clothes, and vinyl records; some sales feature large pieces of

RIGHT: *Martha examines vintage monogrammed linens at an estate sale near her home in Westport, Connecticut.* OPPOSITE: *A collection of hobby horses rests beside a big top at Brimfield, the famous flea market in western Massachusetts.*

furniture or even appliances. No two sales are alike. Most people advertise tag sales in local newspapers (some papers have a special section in the classified ads devoted to them) or on fliers posted around town the week before the event. Sometimes they simply hang a series of signs along the route to the sale from the nearest main intersection. On any given Saturday in July, a typical New England town may have ten or more tag sales going on at once. If you like to drive, you could hit a couple of dozen in one day.

WHAT IS A FLEA MARKET AND HOW CAN YOU FIND ONE?

Flea markets have been around since the Middle Ages, when European towns began holding weekly markets for secondhand goods. The term refers to the insect-ridden merchandise of those early markets. The mother of all flea markets is the Saint-Ouen Marché aux Puces (market of fleas) in Paris, which sprang up on the outskirts of the city in the 1880s and still attracts hordes of shoppers. These days, the term signifies an organized group of merchants who come together for a day, a weekend, or a week to offer their goods to the public. Usually, the vendors set up their tables or stands in a grid, leaving aisles for easy access. Some flea markets are held weekly or monthly. Others are annual or onetime events. Some require no admission fee, but many charge visitors to enter the market or park a vehicle, or both.

More than five thousand flea markets are held each year in the United States, including the forty-dealer boutique affairs held weekly on parking lots in New York City, as well as the giant annual sale that runs for 450 miles along Route 127 through Kentucky, Tennessee, Georgia, and Alabama. Other markets are held in school gymnasiums, in community centers, in fields, and under big circus tents in warmer weather. One of the most famous American flea markets, held in a field at Brimfield, near Sturbridge, Massachusetts, brings together about three thousand dealers for six days every May, July, and September.

Not all flea markets are created equal. Some offer a preponderance of contemporary odd-lot merchandise, such as tube socks, polyester track suits, and plastic toys, or a mixture of new, recently

made, and vintage goods. Before you attend a particular market for the first time, call the organizers and ask what types of goods are likely to be offered. If few vintage dealers are expected and the tube-sock quotient is high, you might want to pass.

Flea-market organizers advertise in local newspapers and on community bulletin boards at post offices and supermarkets. Market locations and organizers may also be listed in the Yellow Pages; certain guidebooks list flea markets that are held regularly throughout the United States. When you are traveling, ask in any antiques shop, or check with the local visitors bureau or chamber of commerce. (In some parts of the country, flea markets are known as swap meets.) And while attending a flea market, ask dealers for the dates and locations of others they know about.

WHAT TO TAKE WITH YOU

CASH: Small bills ($20 or smaller) are best. Traveler's checks are accepted, and some merchants will take personal checks with identification. Few are equipped to take credit cards.

FOOD AND WATER: Some flea markets have food concessions, but unless you like hot dogs and fruit punch, bring your own provisions. Bottled water is a good idea in hot weather.

COMFORTABLE, NONDESCRIPT CLOTHING AND SHOES: Shopping a large flea market requires hours of walking, sometimes over muddy terrain. Bring a sun hat or a rain poncho, sensible shoes or boots, and anything else the weather may require. Don't wear your finest clothes or expensive jewelry or accessories. If you expect to bargain, you will have a hard time convincing sellers that you cannot afford a higher price.

PACKING MATERIALS: It is not unusual for a merchant to have nothing in which to wrap your purchases. Bring bubble cushioning wrap, old blankets, paper bags, newspaper, and tape.

AN EMPTY CAR: Nothing is quite so heartbreaking as finding the perfect pair of tall shutters only to realize you don't have room for them in the car. Empty your vehicle before you come, and don't invite five sightseeing friends—unless they have their own car.

TOOLS: A flashlight comes in handy for early morning forays. A tape measure will help ensure that the piece you've found will fit between your staircase and the kitchen door (measure key spaces in your home before you leave). A magnet may help determine the composition of a find (it won't stick to pure copper or brass but will attach to an iron-based metal that is plated in those materials). A small cart or luggage carrier can help you transport large or heavy items or avoid multiple trips to your car.

HOW TO GET WHAT YOU WANT AT THE PRICE YOU WANT

Bargaining can be fun for the buyer and the seller or unpleasant and unprofitable for both, depending on how you go about it. Remember, flea-market merchants and tag-sale hosts talk all day to a constant stream of strangers who ask questions and relentlessly try to get them to lower their prices. Courtesy and thoughtfulness are the best tools for getting what you want, at a fair price. The following suggestions should help:

DO assume that there is always room to negotiate, but bargain wisely. If you begin by asking a dealer, "What's your best price?" you set yourself up for the reply, "The price marked." Ask instead, "Would you consider taking less for this?"

DO keep your enthusiasm in check. It is hard to bargain once the seller suspects you are going to buy no matter what the price.

DO ask if everything a flea-market merchant has for sale is on display. He may well have other material hidden under his table or still in his truck. If you like the look of his stock and would like to see what else he has, don't be afraid to ask.

DO ask for an overall discount if you wish to buy more than one object at the same time from a merchant. Most are willing to lower prices if they are guaranteed to sell multiple items.

DO inquire about the price range of unpriced box-lot objects (such as silverware) before you make a selection. That way, a shrewd dealer cannot claim that you have chosen the most expensive items in the box and then quote much higher prices.

DON'T contradict a merchant, no matter how much you may know about an object. Insulting the dealer will get you nowhere; listen respectfully, and you might hear some useful information.

DON'T offer an insultingly small amount to start a bargaining session. Your transaction will be finished before it has even begun.

DON'T flash a wad of $20 bills and then ask for $2 off a price. This will likely make the merchant less willing to negotiate.

DON'T belittle the condition of a particular item in hopes of getting a discount. Merchants consider an object's imperfections before pricing, and again, you might make them angry.

DON'T crow over a reduction in price. It makes the merchant look foolish, and you may want to bargain with him another day.

DON'T ask a vendor for free appraisals of antiques or other vintage items that you have brought from home. If you are not interested in buying his wares, it is unfair to draw a merchant's attention away from other customers, especially potential buyers.

DON'T assume that every posted price at a tag sale is a bargain. The seller is not a professional and can ask any price, including a figure that is double or even triple the real value of a piece.

TRICKS OF THE TRADE

Contrary to conventional wisdom, there is no best time to arrive at a flea market or tag sale. It is true that those who arrive the minute the venue opens will find the best selection of goods, but not everybody wants to get up at five o'clock in the morning and hunt around with a flashlight. Some of the worst mistakes are made by people shopping when it is still too dark to see clearly. Also, merchants may not be completely unpacked that early, and they are less inclined to bargain. They have the whole day before them and figure they will surely sell your find to someone else at the full asking price. As the day passes, prices become more flexible. If you hit a sale around four o'clock in the afternoon, you will find less merchandise but better prices. Nobody running a tag sale wants to shove all that stuff back into an already crowded house, and merchants often would rather sell an item at a smaller profit than pack it up and cart it back to their shop. So go when it is convenient for you, and bargain accordingly.

All flea-market veterans have their own modus operandi for covering the territory at a large market. Some start with a quick tour, noting possible goodies, and then circle back to their starting point to buy. Others begin buying immediately rather than take time for an overall assessment, on the plausible assumption that a find may be snapped up by the time they have finished their look around. It is possible to combine these two approaches: Buy anything absolutely wonderful the moment you see it, even if it is on the very first table in a flea market of five hundred dealers, but

leave less-certain purchases until you have had a chance to make the rounds and see what everyone else has to offer.

Buyers are often tempted to pay for something and then ask the dealer to put it aside for them until they have finished shopping for the day. It is far safer to take the item with you immediately. A flea-market merchant may decide to finish early and leave your new purchase unattended, and a tag-sale holder may get a higher offer after you have left and sell your find to that person instead (you will get your money back but lose your purchase). If you absolutely must leave something at a tag sale until later that day, take a piece of it (one drawer of a bureau, for example) with you. That way it is incomplete and unmarketable to others.

It pays to become a regular customer. After you have bought from a particular merchant a few times, he will recognize you as a serious buyer who is likely to buy again. This means he will be inclined to give you more attention and better prices.

Flea markets and tag sales in your neighborhood are just a start. Check out the shopping opportunities when you travel, especially in resort areas. Some of the best selections are found in regions favored by the newly retired, eager to downsize from larger homes and divest themselves of their belongings.

OTHER VINTAGE OUTLETS

As a creative forager, you may wish to shop flea markets and tag sales in spring and summer and spend the colder winter months creating projects with your finds. But if you prefer to shop year-round, here are a few indoor alternatives:

ESTATE SALES are onetime events run by professional organizers to dispose of the contents of a home after its owner's death. A sale is held on-site, usually over several days, and can include nearly everything that the former resident accumulated over a lifetime. Credit cards are often accepted along with cash and checks. It is best to come early to such sales, because only a certain number of people are allowed inside the house at a time. You may have to take a number to get in. Merchandise is organized by type and located in the appropriate part of the house—kitchen items in the kitchen, tools in the garage, linens and clothes in the bedrooms, and china and silver in the dining room. Since you cannot be in every room at once, try shopping in a group. That way, one person can immediately dash to each area and report back to the others on possible finds. Prices are never negotiable on the first day, but if a number of items remain unsold, organizers may become increasingly flexible. Drastic reductions tend to occur on the last day. Estate sales are usually advertised in newspaper classified sections along with local tag sales.

THRIFT STORES are typically established by charitable organizations to sell used clothes, housewares, bric-a-brac, and furniture donated by patrons. Such stores keep regular hours and often

---

FLEA-MARKET JARGON

Vintage-goods merchants have a terminology all their own. Understanding the language will help you communicate—and shop—better.

AS IS: When a merchant marks something "as is," he acknowledges that it is in less than perfect condition and indicates that he has not invested in any repairs. Be sure to inspect "as is" items carefully before you buy.

BRIC-A-BRAC: This is a general term for the small decorative items found in kitchens, living rooms, and bedrooms.

BUCK: Many merchants have an idiosyncratic way of referring to specific amounts of money. If a merchant tells you that the price of a lamp is a buck, he might mean $100. Half a buck may mean $50, and a quarter $25. If in doubt, ask whether he is speaking about dollars or cents.

CIRCA: This Latin word indicates an approximate date for the manufacture of an object. For example, "circa 1890" means it was probably made between 1880 and 1900. The abbreviation is *c.* or *ca.*, as in ca. 1925.

FIRM: If a tag reads "$30 firm," the dealer is telling you he is not prepared to negotiate the price of that particular item in any way.

FOXED: A print or any other piece of paper that has dark blotchy stains is said to be foxed. Such stains, which are due to moisture and age, need to be removed professionally.

HAIRLINE: This refers to a thin crack in a ceramic object. Sometimes a hairline crack is so small you cannot see it, but you will still want to know it is there.

LOT: If items are being sold as a lot, you must buy the whole group; you will not be permitted to pick out the one or two pieces you want and leave the rest.

SMALLS: Merchants who specialize in smalls deal not in furniture but in porcelain, glass, silver, and other tabletop objects. Smalls are usually of higher quality than bric-a-brac.

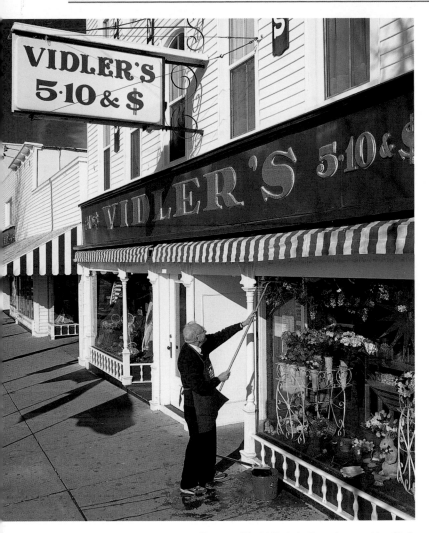

Five-and-dime stores in small towns, like Vidler's in East Aurora, New York, are good sources of vintage fabrics, notions, and tabletop items.

accept credit cards. Goods tend to be grouped by category; all clothing is displayed together, as are all dishes, all picture frames, and so on. Larger stores often carry more furniture than smaller ones, which mostly specialize in garments and bric-a-brac. Items offered are almost always in usable condition, since thrift stores tend not to accept donations in need of repair.

Since most thrift-shop proceeds go to charity, prices are not negotiable, but there are other ways to get good deals. Shops may identify a bargain of the week and mark all shirts $1.50, or reduce all housewares prices every Tuesday. The choicest goods are usually displayed in the window and put on sale gradually to attract a steady flow of customers. Get to know your local thrift store and its ways, and ask a shop attendant exactly how the

pricing system works. Prices for thrift-shop furniture make an excellent benchmark for other vintage shopping. For example, if most used dining-room tables are about $75 and you see one at a flea market for $40, you can be sure you have a find. However, prices at thrift shops in large cities are much higher than those in small, out-of-the-way places. Check out thrift shops whenever you travel, and compare prices from one spot to the next.

CONSIGNMENT SHOPS sell the same types of merchandise as thrift shops, but the proceeds do not go to charity. Everything is sold on behalf of an individual who has consigned it to the shop, which takes a percentage of the selling price in exchange for its services. Quality is usually higher than at thrift shops, as are prices. Consignment shops do not expect bargaining, as they reduce prices on a set schedule. All price tags note the day a piece came in. When an item has remained unsold for a month, the price might be reduced by 10 percent. The next month, it will drop 10 percent more, and so on. Ask the shop owner how the system works, and learn to negotiate it. This can be tricky. Say, for example, that you have your eye on a certain silver platter but have decided to wait until it is reduced by another 10 percent. Only hours after the final reduction, you may find that another customer has beaten you to the punch. If you become a regular, however, a shop owner might be inclined to sell you an item at the lower price just before the next markdown occurs.

SALVAGE YARDS usually have items for sale both indoors and out. They are giant bazaars of vintage architectural parts, where you can find doors, plumbing fixtures, decorative trim, fireplace mantels, fencing, outdoor-lighting fixtures, and garden urns. But be prepared: These are largely do-it-yourself operations. Once the proprietor has shown you where all the doors are (similar items are grouped together), you are on your own. Wear old clothes and boots suitable for muddy ground, and bring along a friend who doesn't mind heavy lifting. If you are looking for something specific, make sure you know the exact dimensions you require. Prices on larger items are usually marked in chalk or grease pencil. Smaller parts, such as knobs, hooks, and hinges, are sorted into boxes according to material or type, with prices marked on the boxes. Although salvage-yard prices are usually

firm, you may be able to negotiate a better overall price if you buy a number of items. Most salvage yards keep regular hours, but it's always wise to telephone ahead to be sure a place is open. A yard owner who gets a call from one of his scouts informing him that a heavily decorated house is about to be demolished may simply close up shop on the spur of the moment and go.

Thrift shops, consignment shops, and salvage yards are all easily located by consulting the Yellow Pages.

A GUIDE TO CREATIVE FORAGING

No matter where you shop, getting yourself in the right frame of mind is the first step to successful foraging. When you are looking for beautiful or well-made finds that can serve a decorative and/or useful purpose, almost anything you see could fill the bill. But making choices in a wide-open field can prove daunting.

One way to sharpen your focus is to keep in mind a list of wants—a holder for the condiments on your table, an inexpensive way to decorate the wall above the couch, a new lamp for the guest room. When something catches your eye, try to envision how it might solve your problem in an attractive and inexpensive way. Could you serve your condiments in that unusual blue-green

pottery planter? Might those crisp linen doilies be framed and arranged on the wall? And what about that graceful old glass pharmacy funnel—could it be converted into a lamp?

On the other hand, sometimes an object simply calls out to you. You have no idea what you are going to do with it, but its curves, texture, or color are wonderfully appealing, and the price is too good to pass up. Take it home. The whole point is to find interesting, affordable objects that speak to you loudly and personally—objects you would like to look at every day. If a find is in that category, you will come up with a use for it.

Not everything that appeals to you is going to be inexpensive. To better focus your search, look most closely at items of minimal interest to the organized collecting world. With a little imagination and work, these bargains can often be transformed into very desirable things indeed. Check out orphans—lone survivors of larger sets. A single teacup or a sugar bowl without a creamer will have a low price, and if the pattern is fabulous, why pass it up? You can put guest soaps or an arrangement of miniature roses in the sugar bowl and plant an African violet in the teacup.

Going against popular taste is another useful gambit: If you happen to like out-of-fashion colors, such as avocado and harvest

gold, you can take your pick of objects other people pass by. When sorting through a pile of monogrammed linens, resist the temptation to search for your own initials. If you don't care whether your own monogram matches the one so beautifully embroidered in white on that set of linen place mats, you could sew them into an elegant, luxurious duvet cover.

Objects no longer usable for their original purpose are wonderful fodder for creative foragers. Few people still plaster the back of their chairs with antimacassars (loose covers that protected upholstery from hair oil—a popular brand of which was Macassar—worn by many men in the nineteenth and early twentieth centuries). But antimacassars are often constructed of fine fabric and can be bought for pennies to be made into a number of useful things or even framed. Similarly, ashtrays have become the dinosaurs of our increasingly smoke-free society, as have silver-plated saucers and tea trays, since few people want to polish them. Fortunately, you can acquire many of these well-shaped pieces for little cash and then put your imagination to work to transform them.

Thinking out of season can also save you money. Prices of many items are influenced by the time of year you are shopping: Everybody looks for watering cans in the summer and woolen blankets in the winter, but you can shop in reverse order instead.

For a decorative display, think in terms of multiples. One dessert mold is nice, but ten of similar shapes and sizes arranged on a kitchen wall is a concept. Almost anything that was made in many patterns or colors is a good bet: doilies, wallpaper samples, baking pans, dish towels, hooks, old bottles—you name it.

HOW TO USE THIS BOOK

The following sections are devoted to the five categories of vintage objects you are likely to encounter at tag sales and flea markets: glass, fabric and notions, kitchenware and ceramics, hardware and salvage, and furniture. Each chapter discusses ways to identify, clean, restore, and care for common finds in that category, then takes you step by step through a series of projects to transform those finds. All required materials and tools are clearly listed, and directions are straightforward and easy to follow.

These projects are only the beginning. Once you are in the creative-foraging frame of mind, you can use our ideas to spark your own strategies for transforming tag-sale and flea-market items. And you'll never again have to pass up something you love because you can't think how in the world to use it.

GLASS HAS LONG BEEN A POPULAR MATERIAL BECAUSE OF THE EASE WITH WHICH IT CAN BE PRODUCED, THE CHEAPNESS OF its raw ingredients, and the beauty of the final product. In the past few hundred years, a surprising number and variety of objects have been made from glass. For domestic use alone, it often shows up on our dining tables as drinking glasses, plates, and serving pieces, as well as atop dressers and mantels in the form of cologne bottles, candlesticks, vases, and boxes. Glass is still used to make storage jars, light fixtures and their shades and bulbs, mirrors, and myriad pieces used in factories, laboratories, automobiles, and shops. As styles change and technology advances, some forms become obsolete or undesirable, and all of these items inevitably make their way to tables at flea markets and tag sales. The extreme fragility of glass means that a significant percentage of all of the pieces manufactured will disappear. However, since so many millions are produced, there is always an excellent selection of survivors from which to choose. For buyers of vintage wares, the previous life of any glass artifact is less important than its shape, size, and inimitable ability to transmit light. This last quality, especially, allows cast-off glass objects to be used in all kinds of creative ways that may have little to do with their original purpose. Whether you are looking for something to reflect or control light, to house living plants, or to show off just about anything, a glass piece may be the answer.

GLASS

HOW GLASS IS MADE

Glass objects are formed by one of two methods: hand-blowing or molding. In the first process, sand is melted at a high temperature to yield silicon. Next, minerals are added either to create or to remove color (glass is naturally a clear aqua). The molten material is then collected on the end of a metal pipe and rolled on a steel table. A glassmaker blows air into the pipe, creating a hollow shape, and continues rolling and blowing until the piece is finished. It is then placed in an oven, where its temperature is reduced very gradually, to avoid cracking.

Molded, or pressed, glass starts out the same way, but instead of being blown on a pipe, the molten material is placed in a metal or ceramic mold. In this way, many identical pieces can be produced quickly. This process became widely used in factories in the mid-nineteenth century. Not surprisingly, hand-blown examples are now much less common. To tell which type of glass you are looking at, check for thickness and the presence of seams: Hand-blown examples are usually thinner than the molded variety and, because they are blown as one piece, have no seams. Pressed glass shows the seams created when molded pieces are joined.

HOW TO DATE A BOTTLE

You can gather important dating information by examining an old bottle. The presence—or lack—of seams will show whether the bottle was blown (dating before 1840), partially machine molded (1840 to 1890), or entirely machine molded (after 1890). The presence of a roundish scar left by the pontil rod (see glossary, opposite) indicates that the bottle was at least partially blown. Commercial markings identifying the producer of the bottle's original contents also help with dating. Eighteenth-century bottles were sometimes marked with a blob of glass (like sealing wax) on which an imprint was made. Nineteenth-century bottles are often embossed with lettering, whereas twentieth-century bottles, which carried paper labels, are more likely to be unmarked.

hand-blown

mold-pressed

machine-made

BEFORE 1840. Bottles were blown and finished entirely by hand. As a result, they exhibit no seams, as there was no mold involved.

1840–1860. In the era of early bottle molds, seaming extended only up to the shoulder. The neck and lip were still finished by hand.

1860–1880. Molds could have several pieces, so the bottle might have more than two seams, which go most of the way up the neck.

1880–1890. Seams end just below the lip, which was now "flash" polished by machine rather than slowly polished by hand.

AFTER 1890. Bottles were made entirely without the touch of human hands, so seams reach all the way to the top, including the lip.

TOP AND CENTER: *Glass markings include (clockwise from top left) strap sides, or shoulder seams left by a mold; a pontil scar, made when the bottle was removed from a pontil rod; whittle marks formed by a newly carved wooden mold; a kick-up bottom, which trapped sediment (as from wine).* **BOTTOM:** *An assortment of vintage glass bottles and jars for sale at a flea market.*

A BOTTLE COLLECTORS' GLOSSARY

PIECE MOLD: A mold constructed of several pieces.

PONTIL ROD: An iron rod attached to the bottom of the bottle (before the blowpipe is removed) to hold the bottle while fashioning the neck or lip. Before the mid-nineteenth century, the pontil rod was attached to the bottle with a blob of hot glass; after the mid-nineteenth century, pontil rods were dipped in powdered iron or lead-oxide and pushed into the bottle.

PONTIL SCAR: The crude roundish mark left on the bottom of the bottle when the end of the pontil rod was broken away; also called an open pontil scar. In bottles that were connected to a pontil rod with powdered iron or lead-oxide, these scars, called iron pontils, may contain metal fragments embedded in the glass.

POLISHED PONTIL: The bottom of a bottle that has been reheated and the pontil scar smoothed until it is invisible. Other makers used a foot-powered grinder to polish the pontil.

STRAP SIDES: Ribs of glass running up both sides of a bottle, creating more pronounced shoulders. Strap sides, also known as strap seams or shoulder seams, were produced by a type of mold that was used in the middle to late nineteenth century.

TURN MOLD: An early nineteenth-century innovation whereby a molded bottle was rotated while still malleable, to erase seams.

WHITTLE MARKS: The impressions left on a bottle that was formed in a carved wooden mold. Usually, whittle marks appear only on the first few bottles formed in a recently carved mold.

AMBER GLASS

The minerals used to create the mellow golden color of this glass are inexpensive enough to have made amber glass a very common material. It was often used in tableware and light fixtures. Because it filters light, it was used for bathroom windows and the transoms above doors in nineteenth- and early twentieth-century houses.

MILK GLASS

Milk glass, formulated with minerals that render it opaque, is made in white and a number of other colors. Jadeite (green) and delphite (blue) were particularly popular between 1920 and 1960 and are popular again today. Milk glass was a frequent choice for makers of tableware, dresser sets, mixing bowls, doorknobs, and lamps.

CRANBERRY GLASS

The mineral required to turn clear glass a vibrant cranberry was pure gold. For this reason, as well as its beauty, cranberry glass has always had a mystique. From the 1850s to the 1950s, it was used to make dresser sets, light fixtures, and tableware of every description. It is often cut, enameled, or painted for even more decorative impact.

MIRROR

Mirror is clear glass backed with a reflective material, which today is chromium, the color of which controls the tint. Up until the end of the nineteenth century, flat glass was extremely difficult to manufacture and to transport. Technological innovations in the late nineteenth century led to its becoming a common household item.

AMETHYST GLASS

There are two kinds of amethyst glass. The first is dyed purple with the addition of specific minerals. The second is clear glass that slowly turns a brilliant amethyst with exposure to direct sunlight. The change is permanent, and the color intensifies the longer the piece is exposed to sunlight.

BEVELED GLASS

Beveling is a technique by which a thick panel of glass is cut, usually on its borders only, to form a decorative pattern. The design gives the appearance of a series of mitered corners. Beveled glass is found most frequently on mirrors but is also used to make tabletops and decorative centerpieces.

MERCURY GLASS

Mercury glass is double-walled and sealed, with silver nitrate trapped between the layers, giving the piece a reflective finish. It can be found in many colors but is most often silver and is thus also known as silvered glass. It is frequently used to make Christmas ornaments, vases, candlesticks, and other decorative tableware.

CUT GLASS

This glass is usually clear and quite thick. It is cut by hand on a grinding wheel into an infinite assortment of decorative patterns. During the last quarter of the nineteenth century, numerous objects were fashioned from cut glass, including lamps, serving bowls, and wine glasses and decanters. Cut glass is still widely produced.

CARING FOR GLASS

Glassware should be washed carefully by hand in tepid water with mild soap. Before you begin, line the sink with a towel to prevent breakage, and if you ordinarily wear a diamond ring, remove it to avoid scratches. Following are tips for cleaning and storing various types of glass:

♦ Clean glass bottles with a bottle brush and warm, soapy water. If that fails to get them completely clean, put some dry rice or ball bearings into the bottles; add warm, soapy water; cover; and shake vigorously. Empty the bottles, and rinse thoroughly.

♦ Undecorated glass may be cleaned by immersion in pure ammonia. This works particularly well for removing food, ink, or the residue of former contents.

♦ Don't use ammonia on glass that is decorated with gilding. Ammonia will oxidize the gold and turn it black.

♦ Avoid using steel-wool soap pads on glass—the metal can scratch the surface. Use a sponge instead.

♦ Glassware that has been washed by machine can develop a stubborn white film on the inside. If your glassware develops this condition, known as sick glass, place it in the dishwasher, pour vinegar and lemon juice in the detergent slot, and run the dishwasher through the normal cycle.

♦ Don't put fine glass in the refrigerator. Sudden shifts in temperature can cause it to crack or break.

♦ Colored glass may become discolored if left too long in direct sunlight. Store yours out of harm's way.

REMOVING PRICE TAGS

PRICE LABELS can seem impossible to remove in any way other than shredding them with a knife or rubbing them with a caustic solution—methods that may harm the underlying surface. In fact, a gentle approach works best: Dip a cotton ball in vegetable oil, and swab the tag until it loosens and falls off. Continue rubbing with oil until any trace of glue is removed, and then wash the object thoroughly.

SIMPLE REPAIRS

Because vintage glass is relatively inexpensive and plentiful, you are better off avoiding any piece that needs repair; hold out instead for a perfect example. If you cannot resist a slightly damaged piece, however, or if an intact object becomes marred in your care, try one of the following repair techniques:

FIXING A BREAK: Use a good-quality epoxy, available at hardware stores. Rinse the broken pieces with water before gluing them. Once they are dry, apply the glue sparingly with a toothpick, using no more than is necessary (the more glue you use, the more visible the repaired break will be). Let the adhesive dry completely (wait at least six hours), and then clean off any excess with acetone and a single-edge razor blade.

FILLING A CRACK: Apply epoxy to fill the inside of the crack, and heat with a hair dryer on a low setting.

SANDING A CHIPPED RIM: Use a jewelers' belt stick, available through jewelry-supply catalogs. Wet the stick, and lightly rub it along the damaged area of the rim until smooth. You can also polish the rim with fine-grained sandpaper or a nail buffer. If the item is one that you intend to display but not to eat or drink from, apply clear nail polish to the surface of the chip. (You may have to repeat this last step periodically.)

VINTAGE MIRRORS

No two vintage mirrors are alike. During a process used in the past to manufacture a sheet of glass, rippling and waviness sometimes occurred as the molten material was being rolled out on a steel table. When the reflective backing was applied, the mirror would then exhibit that same wavy quality.

Mirrors age differently from other glass. As time goes by, the reflective backing wears away, causing subtle streaks and uneven dark spots known as foxing, which give the mirror character. Rather than have a professional restore the backing, enjoy the mirror as is—this foxed appearance is treasured by some vintage-glass collectors. You may even want to speed up the process by spraying ammonia onto the reflective material on the back. A professional can create this look on a new mirror by spraying or brushing a mild acid onto the back of a piece of glass that has been silvered. The surface is then coated with backing paint.

1.

PANELED
mirror

MATERIALS *MIRRORS, GRAPH PAPER, DEEP FRAME, T SQUARE; MASKING TAPE, GLASS CUTTER, PLYWOOD CUT TO FIT FRAME, PAINT STICKS, SUPERGLUE, MIRROR ADHESIVE, GLASS BUTTONS, FINISHING NAILS, LIQUID NAILS, HANGING HARDWARE.* By arranging small mirrors of varying ages and patinas together, you can capture the character and charm of a much larger (and more expensive) antique mirror. **1.** Take the mirrors out of their old frames. **2.** Make a to-scale drawing on graph paper of a simple geometric pattern that will fit into your new frame. **3.** Select a mirror, and then use a T square and masking tape to mark out a section that will fit exactly into one of the pieces in the pattern. **4.** Place the mirror on a flat, towel-covered surface, and, following the directions on the glass-cutter package, cut out the piece. Repeat until all pieces have been cut. **5.** Arrange newly cut mirrors on top of the plywood in the desired pattern according to your graph, and lay the frame on top to make sure everything fits. If the mirrors vary in thickness, equalize thinner ones with pieces of paint stick glued to the corners of their backs. **6.** Turn over a mirror that belongs in one corner of the pattern, and apply mirror adhesive just inside its perimeter and in an X across its center. Press mirror down firmly onto the plywood (on equalized mirror pieces, apply glue on paint-stick pieces at corners). Repeat until all mirror pieces are glued down. **7.** At the juncture of every four corners of mirror pieces, secure glass buttons or rosettes with superglue (see photograph, top left). **8.** When glue dries, turn completed mirror facedown on a flat, towel-covered surface, and secure it to the frame: Use finishing nails and, for extra strength, Liquid Nails applied to outside edge of mirror and inside of frame. **9.** Hang the mirror with an appropriately strong apparatus, attaching the hardware to the plywood backing of the mirror, not just to the frame.

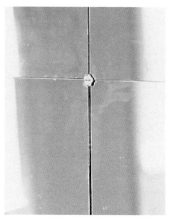

BELOW: *Five-and-dime mirrors in flaky old frames may not look very enticing, but grouping can transform them.* **OPPOSITE**: *Mount inexpensive mirrors in a six-panel grid or another pattern, add glass buttons to the intersections (left), and enclose them in a simple frame. Each mirror will probably have a different waviness and color, reflecting light and people and the room in dreamy, unexpected ways.*

RIGHT: *A pharmacy funnel makes a wonderful display dome for a collection of shells or other small items. These vessels originally dispensed medicines and hung upside down from a harness that fit around the lip of the base, and they are just the sort of object vintage-sale shoppers puzzle over how to reinvent.*

OPPOSITE: *We upended a funnel to make a display dome that doubles as an attractive base for a lamp.*

LAMP COMPONENTS

1	*threaded rod*
2	*socket cap (with hole)*
3	*harp retainer*
4	*locking washer*
5	*nut*
6	*vase cap (with rubber washer)*
7	*vase cap (with rubber washer)*
8	*locking washer*
9	*nut*
10	*cord*
11	*socket body*
12	*plug*
13	*harp*

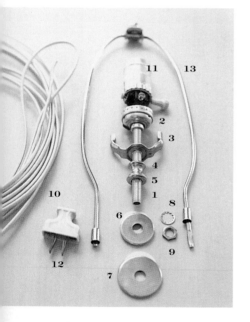

2.
PHARMACY FUNNEL
glass lamp

MATERIALS *THREADED ROD, SOCKET CAP WITH HOLE, HARP RETAINER, LOCKING WASHERS, NUTS, VASE CAPS, RUBBER WASHERS, PHARMACY FUNNEL, LAMP CORD, WIRE STRIPPERS, SOCKET BODY, PLUG, HARP, LIGHTBULB, LAMPSHADE.*

Most pharmacy funnels have very small openings; to convert one to a lamp base, a standard threaded rod must fit through it. If your pinkie finger fits into the funnel's opening, you've found a likely candidate for a lamp. Be sure to measure the funnel neck before you purchase your threaded rod—the rod should be 2 inches longer than the neck. **1.** Loosely thread the threaded rod with a socket cap, harp retainer, locking washer, nut, and vase cap (with a rubber washer already attached), in that order. The vase cap should have a diameter large enough that it sits over the top of the funnel neck. Insert the threaded rod with attachments through the neck of the funnel. **2.** From the wide mouth of the funnel, attach a second vase cap and rubber washer to the threaded rod, so that the vase cap and washer fit inside the funnel against the bottom of neck (which is usually slightly wider than its top). Add another locking washer, then another nut. **3.** Holding the lamp upright (with the neck at the top), thread one end of the cord through the hole in the socket cap. **4.** Using wire strippers, strip ¾ inch of same end of lamp cord, leaving wires exposed; wrap each wire separately to the two screws on the socket body. **5.** Cut cord to desired length on the opposite end; attach cord to plug. **6.** Connect harp to harp retainer. **7.** Attach lightbulb and lampshade. When choosing a shade, it's a good idea to bring the lamp with you to the store.

MATERIALS *GLASSWARE, PLASTIC GLOVES, PHOTOCOPIER, SCISSORS, ADHESIVE-BACKED PAPER, UTILITY KNIFE, MASKING TAPE, PAINTBRUSH, ETCHING CREAM (AVAILABLE AT CRAFTS AND ART-SUPPLY STORES).* To etch glass, wear plastic gloves and long sleeves, and work in a well-ventilated area. Practice on a jelly jar. **1.** Choose a design. The *M* monogram was created with a homemade stencil: Enlarge a piece of text on a photocopier, and cut out one letter. Place it on adhesive-backed paper. Trace the letter, then cut it out with a utility knife, leaving the paper around it intact. We used adhesive hole reinforcements to make polka dots and masking tape to make stripes (glass is etched in areas between or inside the adhesive or tape). **2.** Clean and dry glass. Press design onto glass; rub to make it adhere. **3.** With a paintbrush, apply a thick layer of etching cream where you want the image or design to appear. Apply cream neatly and smoothly and avoid spills, which will leave permanent marks. **4.** Wait 5 minutes, and rinse off cream with warm water.

BELOW AND RIGHT: *Probably the most common offering at tag sales is undistinguished glassware. Take a half-dozen glasses home, and transform them with monograms, stripes, polka dots, or any of countless other patterns achieved with a single application of etching cream. In a matter of minutes, you will have a set of stylish, personalized goblets or rocks glasses.*

4.

BOTTLED
blooms

A LONE FLOWER REVEALS THE PARTICULAR SHAPE OF ITS blossom and line of its stem. Vintage bottles make great show-cases for individual blooms arranged along a windowsill or mantel or clustered on a table. Use a variety of bottles, both clear and tinted, to hold attractive cuttings. If grouping flowers, play with the color palette and texture. You may be attracted to a clean, modern aesthetic, exemplified by this line of clear bottles with white Queen Anne's lace (above), or choose instead to cluster an assortment of wild daisies or black-eyed Susans in old glass inkwells that have lost their caps (right).

LEFT: *Boxes of old milk-glass pieces are common sightings at flea markets. Milk glass has been in production since the early nineteenth century, serving as an inexpensive substitute for more luxurious porcelain tableware. Nowadays, only a handful of companies manufacture milk glass, but because it was mass-produced for more than a century, it remains widely available and affordably priced.*

5.
MILK GLASS
lighting

MATERIALS *MILK GLASS, PLATE HANGERS, WHITE NAIL POLISH, VOTIVE AND SMALL PILLAR CANDLES.* ⚜ A milk-glass plate with lacy openwork (above) casts a beautifully patterned shadow when used as the reflector for a candle sconce. Attach a plate hanger (hanger package will indicate appropriate size) to the back of the plate, and hang it above sconce. (The wire tips of the hanger will virtually disappear if you paint them with white nail polish.) If you want the effect without the sconce, you can hang a plate behind a candlestick on a shelf, cabinet, or mantel, positioning the wick of the candle in the center of the plate. For a warmer glow, shelter candles inside milk-glass vases, compotes, and tumblers (above and opposite). Assemble complementary shapes, textures, and sizes on a mantel, and fill with votive candles. Use a single votive in a bathroom when you have a party, or place it on the bedside table of a guest room before bedtime.

SMALL FRESHWATER GARDENS ARE FUN TO CREATE AND easy to care for. Aquarium suppliers and specialty nurseries sell a variety of plants suitable for growing in water. You can mix them as you please, as long as they like the same growing conditions. For instance, some plants need twelve to sixteen hours of bright light daily, requiring fluorescent grow lights (incandescent lights can overheat water and burn foliage). True aquatic plants such as *Anubias* and parrot feather (*Myriophyllum*) can remain entirely submerged. Other good choices include semiaquatics such as sweet flag (*Acorus americanus*) and umbrella palm (*Cyperus papyrus*), which like only their roots to be submerged; water lettuce (*Pistia stratiotes*) and water hyacinth (*Eichhornia crassipes*), floaters that drift on the surface; and lace plant (*Aponogeton*) and sword plant (*Echinodorus tenellus*), which should be placed in gravel. If using stone or gravel, rinse well to remove dust and salt. You may use tap water, but first leave it in an open container for a day to let any chemicals evaporate. To plant true aquatics, place a layer of stone or gravel in the bottom of the vessel. Fill halfway, then place potted plants directly in the gravel. Use care not to submerge crowns more than ¼ inch. For semiaquatic plants, use shallow containers or a deep layer of gravel to position the crown at the water's surface. Some aquatics have thick roots called rhizomes and may not require soil but will thrive when anchored in a layer of gravel. Floaters, whether submerged or on the surface, may be displayed alone or in combination with other aquatics. Stones can stabilize submerged floaters. After a few weeks, begin fertilizing the plants with tablets made for water gardens (available at nurseries that carry aquatic plants or in aquatic-garden supply catalogs). If the water turns murky, be patient; an initial algae bloom may correct itself. If algae persists, use a natural product such as Pond Saver, available where you buy the plants. Never use soap to clean the glass. Even a trace of detergent in the growing water makes it difficult for a plant to breathe. Some of these plants can be invasive in nature, so it's best not to introduce them into a pond or any other natural habitat.

A vintage glass container can make a good home for a water garden. Use one as a centerpiece, or line a bright windowsill with a series of gardens of different shapes and sizes (opposite). To drain the water without disturbing the plants' roots, set up a siphoning system with plastic tubing, available at aquarium supply stores, and an empty bucket placed at a lower level than the water garden (below).

AS YOU SCOUT THE AISLES OF A FLEA MARKET FOR A suitable terrarium, be on the lookout for a clear glass container with a wide neck for accessibility and a snugly fitting clear glass lid. You want a vessel that will allow light to enter and keep moisture from evaporating. Pharmacy jars, large cookie jars, and commercial candy jars are excellent choices. Start with a 1-inch-deep drainage layer of small stones; aquarium gravel also works well. Top with a light layer of finely ground charcoal (sold with aquarium supplies) to reduce bacterial buildup and help keep the environment fresh. On top of this, place a 3-inch layer of two parts good, dark potting soil; two parts peat; and one part builders' sand mixed together and moistened. Now you are ready to plant: Planting a terrarium is a landscaping opportunity writ small. So think about texture, color, and size when choosing vegetation. Larger plants should be placed in the center to give them room to grow. Collect ferns, stones, and moss-covered twigs on country walks to create a woodland-floor effect, or take inspiration from Japanese gardens and arrange a minimalist bonsai composition with river rocks. Diffused natural light is best for terrariums; direct light is too intense. If sunlight is unavailable, cool or warm fluorescent lights may be used. Lightly water your new terrarium. A day or two later, check to make sure the moisture level is balanced: If a thick fog has settled over the plants, remove the glass lid for a day. If the soil appears parched, however, gently rewater the terrarium and give it a tighter lid. Prune dead leaves and any that grow against the sides—such contact encourages bacterial growth. You can make hanging terrarium gardens (left) for tiny plant specimens such as ficus and ferns, each in its own charmingly shaped old bottle. The bottles are hung with monofilament tied in simple macramé knots and suspended at eye level. Maintain your terrariums with surgical tools.

MATERIALS

1	*suitable terrarium plants*
2	*peat*
3	*potting soil*
4	*moss*
5	*charcoal*
6	*builders' sand*
7	*gravel*
8	*decorative stones*
9	*surgical tools*

LEFT: *Almost any glass container can become its own little world when turned into a terrarium— an enclosed garden that acts as a self-contained ecosystem. Once filled with plants and given a proper balance of light, soil, and water, it will thrive with little attention from you.* **BELOW, FROM LEFT**: *A plant is lowered into a narrow-necked bottle by means of a horseshoe-shaped wire attached to a bamboo garden stake; an old funnel with plastic tubing helps you water one plant that is thirsty when others are fine; if the container has no lid, have a slab of glass cut to fit; a spoon for digging, a cork for tamping soil, and a brush for cleaning the glass sides— tools that can be made from household items—are all attached with waxed twine to handles of bamboo garden stakes.*

8.

JELLY JAR
candles

MATERIALS *WICKS WITH METAL TABS, VINTAGE JELLY JARS, PLUMBERS' OR WICK PUTTY, BLEACHED BEESWAX, DOUBLE BOILER, CANDY THERMOMETER, OIL-BASED ESSENCE.*

Old jelly jars are so easy to come by that we often overlook them. But these sturdy glass containers can be charming and atmospheric in a new role. **1.** Fix a wick to the bottom of a jar using plumbers' or wick putty. **2.** Tie the wick around a pencil so that the wick is taut when the pencil is laid across the top of the jar (below, left). **3.** Place some bleached beeswax (available from crafts stores) in the top of a double boiler. (A pound of beeswax will make four to five candles in 8-ounce jelly jars.) Heat wax to 135 degrees, checking the temperature with a candy thermometer. **4.** Remove the wax from the heat, and stir in about 50 drops of an oil-based essence such as lavender, sandalwood, or jasmine. (The exact amount will depend on the intensity of the scent and your own preference, so keep smelling as you go.) **5.** Pour the newly scented wax into the jelly jars, and set the jars in a room-temperature water bath to cool. Stir gently with a toothpick to avoid any bubbles. Add more wax if the candle falls slightly in the center as it cools. After a candle burns all the way down, put the jar in the freezer briefly. The melted wax will shrink and pop right out (below, right) for easy cleaning.

During the first quarter of the nineteenth century, jelly was sold in glass jars with tin lids and wax seals. Their thick tempered glass withstands heat beautifully, making them the perfect vessels for scented candles. **BELOW**: *Jelly-jar votives are easy to create, and they make wonderful gifts. You'll probably want to keep a few for yourself, so make a dozen or so at a time, in three or four different scents.*

9.

BOTTLED
herb oil

SHOWCASE A COLLECTION OF OLD GLASS DECANTERS BY FILLING THEM WITH HOME-
made infused oils. Olive oil infused with "hard" herbs, such as rosemary, thyme, sage, oregano, savory, and bay leaves, is ideal for salads. Begin by cleaning your glass bottles with warm, soapy water. To dry (right), tightly roll a paper towel, and insert it three-fourths of the way into the bottle; it will absorb the moisture. (Don't air-dry; the water only condenses and becomes trapped, eventually discoloring the glass.) To make the oil, first set aside several of the prettiest leaves or sprigs of 1 cup of fresh herbs for garnish, and then combine remaining herbs with 2 cups of extra-virgin olive oil in a saucepan over medium heat. Heat just until the herbs start to sizzle (do not let the oil smoke). Remove from heat, and let oil cool before discarding the herbs. Pour the oil into the bottles. Submerge reserved sprigs in the oil (they will eventually mold if not completely covered). A piece of string tied around the herb stem makes removal easy once the oil no longer covers them. Cork or seal the bottles. Display decanters in a cool, dry place away from sunlight. Refrigerate for long-term storage.

THE HURRICANES KEEPING THESE VOTIVE CANDLES SAFE FROM FLAME-SNUFFING breezes were designed as chimneys or shades for oil lamps in the late nineteenth century and for electric light fixtures a few decades later. These days, you might find whole collections of them, like the ones at left, at second-hand shops and tag sales, usually for less than $10 apiece. Keep an eye out for subtle nuances in color—even white glass often has a slight tint, the result of varying amounts of silica sand and other ingredients. Transparent chimneys that display wavy striations and air bubbles trapped in the glass during the blowing process may refract light beautifully. To use a chimney as a hurricane, place a votive candle on a saucer, light it, and cover it with the glass. Consider grouping chimneys and saucers in various colors and shapes to provide soft lighting for any space.

11.

FRUIT JAR
storage

EVEN IF YOU AREN'T IN THE HABIT OF PUTTING UP GALLONS OF HOMEMADE PRESERVES, you may want to stock up on a few vintage canning jars for organizing odds and ends. Sturdy and transparent, they provide easy access to picture-hanging paraphernalia, the pennies that accumulate in your change purse, desk accoutrements such as stamps and pens, or, in the bathroom, a month's worth of fluffy cotton balls. Vintage fruit jars come in blue, amber, olive green, and other colors, as well as clear. Some have metal or glass lids, originally designed to preserve freshness. The imposing topper on the right (above) is called a claw-and-glass-patch lid. It covers an 1861 Whitall jar.

shrinking inclination to iron fine linens, work in the secondhand shopper's favor. The vintage market's supply of well-made, inexpensive textiles—in the form of curtains, tablecloths, dish towels, dresser scarves, bed linens, and clothing—is almost unlimited, and so are the many innovative ways to put them to use. When you spot a piece that appeals to you, look beyond its original household category. Focus on the color, pattern, and texture to envision new ways the piece can be incorporated into your home. A few men's wool suit jackets can be cut into squares and sewn together to make a handsome quilt; likewise, a set of fine linen hand towels might hang beautifully as privacy curtains. If you have a specific project in mind, be sure a piece of fabric is the appropriate size, weight, and strength. Wool is too heavy for a lampshade, for example, and silk fabrics may not be strong enough to upholster a chair. But remember that fabric is by nature impermanent. If your find has already had one full life, it may last only another five or ten years. Acknowledge its life span and enjoy it, however long it may last. Notions— often offered alongside vintage textiles—can be equally inspirational: Suspend a small framed print from a ribbon anchored with a large decorative button, or transform a Bakelite or tortoiseshell belt buckle into a picture-frame refrigerator magnet.

Fabric & Notions

Vintage buttons are usually found in buckets or bins, but sometimes an intact card turns up. This French example is from a market in upstate New York.

NOTIONS

Notions are the small add-ons of the fabric world—the closures and trimmings that are often sold alongside textiles. Vintage buckles, buttons, frog closures, ribbons, braid, and trimmings of all kinds are often more beautiful than their modern counterparts. Look under the lids of the tins and boxes that accompany piles of linens and dish towels at a flea-market merchant's stand. That's where you may uncover interesting or unusual fabric-related items. Sometimes these small treasures will be sorted by type, but more often you will have to sift through a mishmash of buttons and buckles or unwind a mixed skein of ribbons and trimmings.

Although appealing, early plastic buttons may decay and fall apart with age because the celluloid of which so many were made is less durable than later synthetics. Rubber buttons, too, have been known to dry out and become unusable. Look instead for buttons made of shell, wood, or bone. They are the most durable and often are beautifully carved. Hang them at the end of window-blind sashes, or let them punctuate the tufting of upholstery. However, don't put them on any clothes you plan to dry-clean or run through the washing machine. Both processes can destroy old buttons.

Look for trim and braid in luxurious materials or interesting colors, and use them to personalize guest towels or give curtains a custom look. Since notions are available in abundance at any vintage sale, don't settle for broken, discolored, or torn items. A perfect example is probably waiting around the corner.

IDENTIFYING FABRICS

To properly use, clean, or store a vintage fabric, it helps to know what you are dealing with. If you look through enough piles at tag sales and flea markets, you will learn to distinguish one fiber and weave from another. For example, rayon and silk are often both shiny and slick, but rayon is generally heavier. Linen is a stronger, more durable fabric than cotton. Use your memory to try to establish a time frame for the item in front of you, since dating it may hint at the type of fabric it's made of: Maybe your mother bought a similar dish towel for her kitchen in 1972. An article made before the sixties is more likely to be cotton than

COMMON FINDS AND FABRICS		
TABLECLOTHS NAPKINS	}	cotton, rayon, or linen
DISH TOWELS SHEETS AND BEDDING	}	cotton or linen
ANTIMACASSARS DOILIES DRESSER SCARVES HANDKERCHIEFS	}	cotton, linen, or silk
CHENILLE BEDSPREADS	}	cotton
BLANKETS	}	wool or cotton
NECKTIES	}	silk, rayon, or wool
MEN'S SUITING	}	wool, cotton, or rayon
RUGS	}	wool, nylon, or cotton

COTTON

DAMASK

DAMASK
with openwork

FUSTIAN

FELT

LACE

LINEN

HOMESPUN LINEN

LINEN
with openwork

BELGIAN LINEN
with appliqué

MATELASSE

RAYON

SATIN

SILK

VELVET

WOOL

a synthetic imitation. On the other hand, rayon has been around since the thirties, so it's never safe to assume that a silky fabric from the forties or fifties is the real thing.

CLEANING AND STAIN REMOVAL

Before you purchase a vintage item made of fabric, take the following precautions: Equip yourself with plastic garbage bags when you go shopping, and seal a suspicious find before you bring it home and risk pest infestation. To kill moths, dry-clean the item or expose it to direct sunlight for at least six hours. For other pests, dry cleaning is a surefire remedy (though be aware that dry-cleaning chemicals may damage very fragile fabric).

The following guidelines will help you determine how to care for a particular fabric once you have purchased it.

COTTON AND LINEN

✦ Most linen and cotton items may be washed by machine in cold water on the gentle cycle, but assume that an old fabric has not been exposed to water for a long time, and proceed with caution. Soak linen or cotton in cold water for twenty-four hours to rehydrate the fibers before you begin any other cleaning process.

✦ Small machine-washable items, such as hand towels or handkerchiefs, should be laundered inside a stocking or pillowcase to keep them from becoming mangled.

✦ Tablecloths and bed linens can be bleached by spraying them with a solution of lemon juice and water and laying them on the grass in the sunshine. Smaller white items, such as handkerchiefs, napkins, and pillowcases, may be boiled on the stove in a solution of four parts water and one part bleach. Never use even a small amount of bleach on anything embroidered with colored thread, however, because it will remove the color.

✦ Large, heavy items should not be line-dried, as they may stretch. Instead, lay them flat to retain the shape.

✦ Don't be afraid to soak cotton or linen for a long time. Soak a stained item in Clorox II or Biz for up to a month, changing the water every couple of days. You can also try boiling it on the stove in a mixture of water and Cascade dishwasher crystals. As a final solution, rub the stain with a toothbrush covered in Wisk or

Goop, an industrial-strength hand cleaner (don't use these last two products on valuable articles, but if you have paid very little and all else has failed, they are worth a try).

✦ To camouflage the yellowing or staining of white fabric, consider tea dyeing. Tea gives fabric a warm beige hue and masks any discolorations. Clean the fabric (but don't use bleach) before you begin. To make the dye, bundle tea leaves in a square of cheesecloth, tie loosely with twine, and immerse in a pot of boiling water. (We recommend a ratio of six cups water to one cup tea.) Add one tablespoon of alum (an inexpensive chemical widely available at drug stores in both granular and powdered forms), which will set the color. Let the tea steep for ten to fifteen minutes, strain the tea (wear rubber gloves to squeeze the cheesecloth bundle), and remove any leaves that float to the surface of the water. Fabric should be thoroughly wet before you add it to the dye solution. Submerge the cloth in the dye, stirring occasionally, until it has taken on the desired color. (The color will lighten as it dries.) One laundering will remove any odor from the tea.

OTHER FABRICS AND FINISHES

CROCHET OR LACE: Don't put these fabrics in the washing machine. Wash them by hand with a mild detergent and water, and use the stain-removal methods recommended for cotton or linen. To dry lace or crochet, lay it on a board, stretch it taut, and anchor it with nails to preserve its shape. If an item has a string hanging from it, do not pull it; you might unravel the rest of the pattern. Instead, knot the string at its source and cut the end.

FRINGE: Knotted fringe on a towel or tablecloth should be washed and combed straight with a plastic fork, dog-grooming brush, or wide-toothed comb before drying.

RAYON: If a rayon item is badly stained, assume it may stay that way, since it is much more difficult to clean than other natural fibers. Take a chance and have it dry-cleaned if it is inexpensive.

SILK AND WOOL: These fabrics should usually be dry-cleaned. You can, however, machine-wash wool blankets in Woolite and cold water on the delicate cycle, then put them in the dryer on a low heat setting for five minutes (this helps shape the weave without shrinkage). Then lay them flat until completely dry.

OPPOSITE: *Bolts of fabric are among the more popular finds at flea markets. A large quantity of vintage fabric provides almost unlimited scope for sewing projects like slipcovers and upholstery, and because this yardage has never had another life, it will be particularly durable.*

LEFT: *The presence of an initial or a monogram on hand towels like these usually signifies top-quality fabric, but the specific letters do not necessarily matter. If you think of a monogram simply as a pleasing graphic design, you can make it work for you.*

CARE AND STORAGE

✦ Light can be the enemy of fine fabrics. If a piece is already old, don't accelerate deterioration by exposing it to constant sunlight. Rotate curtains made of vintage fabric, and put away your vintage duvet or bedspread for part of the year to reduce wear.

✦ Don't store wool fabric directly against a wooden shelf or drawer bottom. Chemicals in the wood accelerate the deterioration of the fabric. Wrap the item in acid-free tissue before putting it away, and line your shelves and drawers with more tissue.

✦ Long-term folding will cause yellowing and wear along creases. Roll large items around wrapping-paper tubes, and store smaller ones flat. Wrap all fabric in acid-free paper before storing. To protect a particularly fragile item, such as a needlepoint sampler, roll it in linen. Make sure it doesn't touch cardboard or wood or anything with chemicals that might cause deterioration.

PROJECT DOS AND DON'TS

DO match like with like. Dissimilar weaves and textures will look odd when mixed. For example, use only similarly woven wool pieces in a patchwork duvet, all-linen hand towels to upholster a hassock, or pure-silk ties to make a lampshade.

DO take a closer look at dirty or yellowing tablecloths or napkins. Such wear often appears only along the folds of long-stored items, and the rest may be clean and white. Cutting away yellowed areas may leave many pieces of good-quality fabric.

DO think unconventionally. Turn a tablecloth with a pretty border into a lampshade, or use a thick wool carriage blanket as a rug. Use the salvageable parts of damaged Navajo or Oriental rugs to make pillows or to upholster a chair seat.

DO note that most silks and wools are dry-clean-only fabrics, and factor in this cost when you are evaluating a find.

DON'T let small stains or discolorations discourage you from taking home a selection of elegant linens. Many stains can be easily boiled or soaked away, and if a discoloration does persist, you can always camouflage it by tea-dyeing.

DON'T use vintage silk for any project requiring strength. It can be very fragile and may suddenly shred.

DON'T be afraid of small holes or damaged fabric edges. Usually you can work around them quite easily.

OTTOMAN
slipcover

MATERIALS *OTTOMAN, FABRIC, SEWING SCISSORS, DRESS-MAKERS' CHALK, PIPING (OPTIONAL), SEWING MACHINE.* Don't hesitate to use several coordinating colors and patterns for the slipcover—a reversible damask would be an attractive choice—but choose just one kind of fabric (cotton, rayon, linen) for each project. **1.** Measure the area of the top of the ottoman. Cut a piece of fabric to this measurement, adding a 1-inch seam allowance. **2.** Measure perimeter of ottoman. Cut four pieces of fabric for the upper side band, allowing for 1-inch seams. **3.** For the lower band, cut one continuous piece 25 inches longer than the perimeter measure (the extra length is for corner pleats and seam allowance). The width of the bottom band is determined by how low you want the cover to hang. **4.** Place top piece on ottoman, wrong side out, and pin the four upper-side-band pieces to it, right sides together, until cover fits as you desire. Match corner seams to corners of ottoman. With chalk, mark seams to guide stitching. **5.** Remove fabric from ottoman, and take pieces apart. Repin corner seams, and stitch upper band together. Repin upper band to ottoman top with piping (if using) between right sides of fabric. Using zipper foot, stitch seams as close to piping as possible. Trim seams and notch corners. **6.** Fit sewn-together part of slipcover over ottoman, wrong side out. Pin ends of lower band together. Placing that seam about 1 inch from a corner of the upper band, pin the two bands together (wrong side out) for 1½ inches along their horizontal seam on either side of corner. **7.** To make a pleat: Fold 1½ inches of lower band back on itself, then fold again in opposite direction, accordion-style; pin in place. Repeat on opposite side of corner. You should now have two 1½-inch pleats that meet precisely at the corner. Repeat at each corner, adjusting to fit as you go. **8.** Mark seams, unpin fabric, and sew pleats and vertical lower-band seam. Then repin lower band to upper band with piping in place, if using. Stitch. **9.** Hem skirt to desired length.

ABOVE: *Vintage fabrics are so plentiful and inexpensive that you should have no trouble gathering an armful of designs and colors that will look good together. Tablecloths, bed covers, napkins, table runners, and pillowcases are all good choices.* **OPPOSITE**: *Make a sofa's worth of throw pillows with your fabric finds, or give a room a fresh look by slipcovering an ottoman.*

2.

VINTAGE FABRIC
pillows

MATERIALS *FABRIC, SEWING SCISSORS, SEWING MACHINE, WELTING FABRIC (OPTIONAL), COTTON CORDING (OPTIONAL), PILLOW INSERT.* The pillow covers shown opposite are all variations on the basic knife-edge pillow. **1.** To make a knife-edge pillow cover, you will need two pieces of fabric of equal dimensions—the length and width of the pillow cover plus ½ inch all around for the seam allowance. A 16-inch square pillow cover, for example, requires two 17-inch squares of fabric. Use the same fabric for both pillow sides, or choose complementary designs. **2.** If you're not adding piping, pin together both fabric pieces with right sides facing and edges aligned. Sew the fabric together along three sides, ½ inch from the edges. Turn right side out, and press. Insert pillow, then close the fourth side with a slip stitch. **3.** To make piping for your pillow cover, cut piping fabric (use the same type of material as the pillow cover in a contrasting color) on the bias into 2-inch-wide strips. If you expect to wash a pillow cover, preshrink any piping fabric made of cotton or linen by washing it several times; this will also prevent its dye from bleeding onto the pillow. **4.** Sew the strips end to end to make a length equal to that of the diameter of the pillow cover plus a 1-inch seam allowance; a 16-inch square pillow cover requires 65 inches of piping. Fold the strip (right side out), with raw edges even, around an equal length of ¼-inch cotton cording. **5.** Using the zipper foot on your sewing machine, stitch along the length of the strip as close to the cording as possible to ensure a snug fit. Trim raw edges to ½ inch from the seam. Pin the piping to the right side of one of the pillow cover pieces, so the raw edges are flush and rounded edge lies toward the center of the piece of fabric. **6.** Where the piping rounds the corners, notch the seam allowance so the piping lies flat. Overlap ends. Stitch in place, following the seam line on the piping. **7.** Lay the second piece of pillow-cover fabric over this piece, right sides facing; pin. Stitch around three sides. Trim corner, turn right side out, and press. Insert pillow. Close the fourth side with a slip stitch.

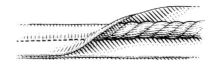

FABRIC-COVERED PIPING

OPPOSITE: *These three pillow covers are made from cotton tablecloths and fabric remnants in colors chosen to coordinate with the ottoman's slipcover. The top pillow, made of red-and-white striped fabric, is backed with white seersucker. The bright piping on the middle pillow accentuates the former tablecloth's pink, red, and white floral design. The bottom pillow is the simplest in form, although the interlocking stripes of the fabric's pattern lend it graphic interest.* **ABOVE**: *To add piping to a pillow cover, fabric-covered cotton cording is stitched to its perimeter.*

MOST CARRIAGE BLANKETS ARE THICKER AND HEAVIER than ordinary blankets because they were made to keep travelers warm in unheated vehicles. That sturdiness, along with their geometric or striped patterns, makes them perfect as area rugs. We added layers of bump (an industrial felt available at carpet stores) and canvas to help our rug lie flat. Cut out pieces of bump and canvas 2 inches narrower than the blanket on its long sides. Turn 1 inch of each long blanket edge over, and slip-stitch all three layers together. Place the blanket on a nonslip rug pad.

4.

WOOL SUIT
blanket

THIS PAGE: *A thick carriage blanket in a pleasing plaid or stripe (left) is easily transformed into a soft area rug (above). Adding layers of canvas and industrial felt (below) helps the rug lie flat and hold its shape.* **OPPOSITE:** *A few men's suits can be fashioned into a handsome throw. Our pattern alternates the darkest gray with a light gray on one row and dark with medium grays on the next.*

MATERIALS *THREE TO FOUR WOOL SUITS, IRON, GRAPH PAPER, CARDBOARD, ADHESIVE-BACKED SANDPAPER, DRESS-MAKERS' CHALK, COTTON BROADCLOTH OR OLD SHEET (FOR INTERLINING), WOOL FLANNEL (FOR BACKING), YARN.* Take clothing apart at the seams, remove lining, and iron it flat before proceeding. **1.** Sketch pattern on graph paper. **2.** Cut out a 5-inch-square cardboard template (the finished squares will be 4½ inches). Back the corners of one side of template with adhesive-backed sandpaper so it won't move while you trace. **3.** Using chalk, trace squares onto clothing pieces, placing them close together and aligned with the fabric grain. Cut out squares (this 40-by-58-inch throw used 117). **4.** Pin squares in rows. Stitch squares together, using a ¼-inch seam allowance; press seams. **5.** Pin rows together, matching seams; stitch, using a ¼-inch seam allowance. Press seams. **6.** Cut lining and backing to fit patchwork. Pin patchwork to backing with right sides facing, then pin the interlining to the patchwork (this throw required 1½ yards of 60-inch-wide fabric). Stitch all the way around, leaving a 10-inch opening on one side. **7.** Clip corners, turn inside out, and press. Hand-stitch to close. **8.** Thread a large needle with a length of yarn, and make a stitch at every corner. Tie stitches into knots on the right side.

= 5. =

HANDKERCHIEF
curtain

MATERIALS *HANDKERCHIEFS, SEWING MACHINE, CAFE CUR-TAIN RINGS, TENSION ROD.* ☙ The transformative properties of a magician's handkerchief are well known, but vintage hankies can bewitch too, when fashioned into a café curtain. **1.** Determine how many handkerchiefs you will need to cover the bottom half of a window (six, sewn edge to edge in two rows, fit this window perfectly). **2.** Join handkerchiefs with a zigzag stitch. If necessary to fit your window, evenly overlap the edges before sewing. **3.** Attach curtain to clips on café curtain rings (available at hardware stores), and hang the curtain from a tension rod.

= 6. =

FRAMED
handkerchiefs

MATERIALS *HANDKERCHIEFS, GLASS, POSTER BOARD, SWISS CLIPS, FOIL TAPE, PICTURE WIRE.* ☙ Before the 1960s, many handkerchiefs were printed with attractive geometric designs. Framed and grouped on a wall, they become pleasing decoration for any room. **1.** Wash and iron handkerchiefs; measure each of the four sides, and add ½ inch to each measurement. **2.** Have ⅛-inch-thick glass and ¹⁄₁₆-inch-thick poster board cut to these dimensions for each handkerchief. **3.** Center each handkerchief on its poster board, and cover with glass, matching up the edges. Do not use tape or glue to mount the handkerchief, as residue from either can stain or discolor the fabric. **4.** Fasten a Swiss clip to the middle of one side to secure frame while you apply foil tape (available at framing stores; see photograph, right) to enclose the opposite edge, making sure the tape adheres to both the front and the back. Snip foil tape at the corners. Attach another Swiss clip to the center of each side of the frame. The clips provide the hardware to attach picture wire for wall mounting.

Paper tissues were invented in 1924, and shortly thereafter, linen handkerchiefs began to fall out of use. A box of folded handkerchiefs at a vintage clothing store might not look promising, but each cloth square, unfolded, can be a work of art (opposite), or they can all be sewn together to make a window curtain (above). If you are planning to frame your handkerchiefs, look for patterns and colors that harmonize, or choose a dominant color or pattern. Simple, semi-transparent linen handkerchiefs work best for a café curtain.

=== **7.** ===

TEA TOWEL
shoulder guards

MATERIALS *TEA TOWELS, SEWING SCISSORS, GROMMETS AND GROMMET PUNCH, HAMMER,*
CLOTHES HANGERS. ✻ To keep hanging garments free from dust, drape them with washable
tea-towel shoulder guards. Choose assorted colors and patterns of tea towels. You'll need to add a
½-inch grommet to the center of each towel so it can be slipped over a hanger hook: Fold the towel
in quarters, and make a small hole by snipping off only the very point of the corner. Unfold, and
attach grommet. Put clothes on hanger, then slide shoulder guards over the hook.

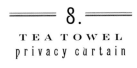

8.
TEA TOWEL
privacy curtain

MATERIALS *DISH OR TEA TOWEL, JUMP RINGS, CUP HOOKS.* A dish or tea towel secured to the window frame allows the window to be raised while the curtain stays in place. Look for a towel that is either the height or the width of the windowpane (towels can be hemmed to the right size, or if you happen to find a bolt of toweling, make several curtains at once). A towel with a woven border looks more curtainlike, but any pattern will do. **1.** Sew jump rings (available at any crafts or jewelry-supply store) to the top corners of each towel, looping thread over corners and into hem to hide the finishing knots. **2.** Screw cup hooks into the window frame, aligning them where the top of the curtain will start, and slip jump rings over the hooks. The curtain will fall precisely into place, letting in plenty of light but obscuring the bottom half of the window.

LEFT: *Vintage dish or tea towels don't have to languish in the kitchen drawer. Transform them into privacy curtains, and you will have a simple, attractive way to finish a bathroom or kitchen window.* **BELOW**: *Jump rings and cup hooks keep the curtain taut while it hangs in the window.*

MATERIALS *DAMASK TEA TOWEL WITH FRINGE, SEWING MACHINE, IRON, PILLOW INSERT.*
Flea-market merchants often sell interesting unused textiles, such as these damask tea towels, which
we turned into covers for a set of throw pillows arranged on a window seat. Making these pillow
covers is so simple, you'll want to make several at once. For the two square pillows, we used
towels that each measure 21 by 37 inches. Choose sizes appropriate for your pillow inserts.
1. Lay the tea towel right side up, and fold it in half, so that the fringed edges meet. (This makes
the finished size of our pillows 20½ by 18½ inches.) Pin top and bottom layers of fabric together
along the unfringed edges. **2.** Stitch the two side seams, using a ¼-inch seam allowance. Press seam
allowances open. **3.** Turn the pillow cover right side out, and press side seams. **4.** Insert your pillow,
and close the open end of the cover by hand, using a slip stitch.

RIGHT: *Three pillows covered with
damask tea towels add a nice decorative touch to this cozy corner by
the window. The rectangular pillow
cover requires a damask towel
for the front and a plain tea towel
for the back. Square pillow covers,
like the two pictured here, are made
by simply folding tea towels in half.*

MATERIALS FOR SEAT COVERS *SCREWDRIVER, CRAFT PAPER, TABLECLOTH WITH INTACT BORDER, SEWING SCISSORS, STAPLE GUN.* ❧ A standard tablecloth should cover four standard dining chairs. **1.** Remove seats from chairs by unscrewing them at the corners on the underside. **2.** Trace a seat onto craft paper to make a template; mark center of template for placement of the border pattern. **3.** Place template over tablecloth; add 3 to 4 inches of fabric on all sides, then cut. **4.** Lay fabric facedown. Lay seat facedown on top, centering pattern. Stretch fabric tightly around seat. **5.** Staple fabric on back of seat evenly all around so it doesn't pucker or pull. Begin at centers of opposite sides; continue with other sides, working toward corners and pulling fabric evenly. **6.** Replace covered seat in frame.

MATERIALS FOR LAMPSHADE *TABLECLOTH WITH INTACT BORDER, SEWING SCISSORS, 16-INCH-DIAMETER WIRE RING, SEWING MACHINE, GROMMETS, GROMMET PUNCH, THREE OR FOUR LIGHTWEIGHT CHAINS, NEEDLE-NOSE PLIERS, CUP HOOKS.* ❧ **1.** Cut a strip of the tablecloth's border approximately 13 to 14 inches wide, plus 1¼ inches for seam allowance, with border centered. The length will depend on how much of a ruffle you want: For a straighter shade, the length should equal the ring's circumference plus ½ inch for seam allowance; for a fuller shade, it should be 1⅓ to 1½ times the circumference plus ½ inch. One long edge is the finished edge of the cloth. For the other edge, turn under ¼ inch of fabric; fold again and stitch to make a 1-inch-wide channel at the top. **2.** Slip ring through channel at top, and play with fullness until you get the look you want. **3.** Cut finished strip to desired length, and stitch ends together to form a loop. **4.** To hang shade, put four small grommets at regular intervals through fabric at top, just under the ring. **5.** To attach chains, open the first link with needle-nose pliers, and close around wire frame and through grommets. The length of the chains will depend on your ceiling height and the desired drop of the shade. **6.** Insert cup hooks in the ceiling plate around the fixture canopy to hold up each chain.

THIS PAGE: *Pick up a vintage tablecloth with a woven or printed border at a flea market, then get out your sewing scissors. You can center the linear pattern on a set of chair seats (above) or a hanging lampshade (right) to give your kitchen or porch a new look. Make the shade by bending a length of stiff wire into a ring, or use a single-wire wreath form.*

BELOW: *Now that most luggage is soft-sided and collapsible, vintage hard leather, cardboard, or fabric-over-cardboard traveling bags from the 1930s through the 1950s are easy to find, although their linings are often ripped or heavily worn.*
RIGHT: *Line a suitcase with vintage fabric, and then equip it with flatware, plastic dishes, and a thermos for all of the amenities of a nostalgic movable feast.*

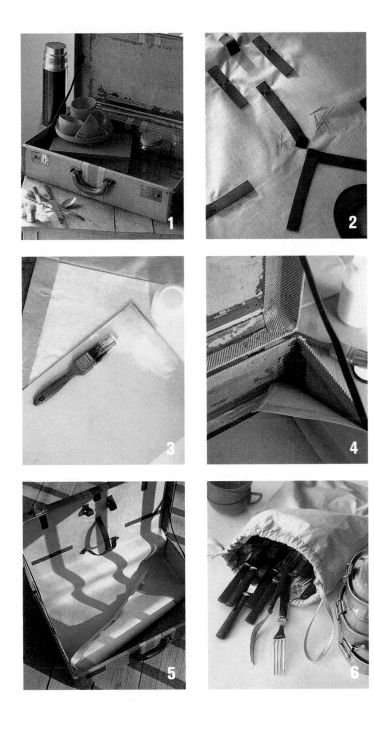

MATERIALS *SUITCASE WITH WORKING LOCKS AND A STRONG HANDLE, TAPE MEASURE, SEWING SCISSORS, FABRIC, FUSIBLE INTERFACING, SPRAY STARCH, RAYON-BLEND ELASTIC TAPE, VELCRO, BOOK BOARD, GLUE BRUSH, HOT-GLUE GUN, WATER-REPELLENT SPRAY, OILCLOTH (OPTIONAL), OXFORD CLOTH (OPTIONAL).* You can use any type of durable fabric to line a suitcase hamper; a vintage tablecloth or checked bedspread looks particularly charming. **1.** Rip out the old lining of the suitcase. To line the case, measure from the front of the top lid to the front of the bottom; add 1-inch seam allowances on all sides, then cut a length of sturdy fabric to this measurement. Strengthen the fabric with fusible interfacing, available at sewing-goods stores; add an extra layer of interfacing where the fabric will drape loosely over the hinge connecting the lid and bottom. Stiffen the lining with spray starch. **2.** To create loops for flatware and a harness for plates, pin strips of rayon-blend elastic tape to the lid lining where utensils will be kept, and, at the center, form an upside-down Y using three strips of tape. Double-stitch tape to fabric. We used Velcro to secure the harness where the ends of the tape meet, but a snap would also work. **3.** Cut a piece of book board to fit snugly inside the lid of the case. Glue lid-lining fabric to the board, smoothing as you go; fold and glue seam allowance onto back of board. Weight board with a few heavy books, and let dry overnight. **4.** Using elastic tape, create hinges for hamper sides, and hot-glue them in place. Cut panels of lining fabric for the hamper sides, adding 1-inch seam allowances. Hem top edges of the panels, miter the bottom corners, and glue to sides. **5.** Glue lid lining to hamper, covering lid hinge ends. Weight and dry overnight. Glue bottom lining to hamper, leaving section between lid and bottom free. Weight and dry overnight. Treat lining with water-repellent spray. **6.** To hold spare utensils, make a pouch lined with oilcloth. Napkins with simple roll-down hems can be made of oxford cloth. Flatware and plates fit in elastic holders and harness. Cups, food tins, and napkins fit snugly in the bottom of the case.

Not so long ago, fashionable belts, especially those on coats, bore all sorts of pretty buckles. When the garments wore out or went out of style, frugal housewives saved the buckles for reuse. Now that these buckles are less in demand as dressmaker details, they are free, with slight modification, to take on new roles as miniature picture frames. Arrange the curios on a bureau (opposite), or display them as refrigerator magnets (right).

12.
BELT BUCKLE
frames

MATERIALS *BUCKLES, PHOTOGRAPHS, COLOR PHOTOCOPIER, DREMEL ROTARY TOOL AND ATTACHMENTS, CARD STOCK, ARCHIVAL DOUBLE-SIDED TAPE OR GLUE, PAINTBRUSH, ADHESIVE MAGNETIC SHEETING (OPTIONAL).* **1.** Look for buckles made of abalone, wood, metal, or Bakelite with a sizable opening. **2.** Choose a graphically bold photograph, such as a close-up portrait, that will read from a distance. Make a color photocopy, reducing it if necessary. **3.** Remove the buckle's center bar with a Dremel rotary tool and a No. 409 cutting wheel. With tool set on low, cut a section from the middle of the center bar, leaving about ¼ inch at each end to prevent chipping. Then fit the Dremel with a No. 932 grinding stone, and abrade away the rest of the bar. You may use vise grips padded with cloth to hold the buckle steady. **4.** Trace the outside of the buckle onto card stock. Cut out shape to form the backing. Attach photocopy to backing with archival double-sided tape or archival glue. With a small paintbrush, apply glue to the front edges of the photocopy, press it to the buckle, and weight it with a few books. Let dry for at least 8 hours. To magnetize the frame, cut strips of adhesive magnetic sheeting and affix them to the back.

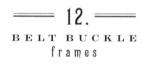

ABOVE: *Display beautiful old doilies on a wall rather than locking them in a drawer. Choose a mat the same color as the wall on which a doily will be hung, and the design will appear to be suspended in air.* **LEFT**: *Juxtapose small, individually framed doilies of similar shapes. We used coordinating shades of green for the matting and simple birch frames.* **BELOW**: *A selection of doilies at an estate sale.*

F R A M E D
d o i l i e s

LACE DOILIES ONCE DECORATED VICTORIAN DRESSERS and shielded the backs of parlor chairs from both wear and Macassar oil, the messy men's hairdressing that gave antimacassars their name. Then ornate trim on furniture went out of style, and doilies were put away in storage trunks and drawers. Today, stacks of them turn up on flea-market tables and at estate sales. Their repeating geometric patterns have a strong graphic appeal that makes them perfect for framing. If a cotton or linen doily is soiled, hand-wash it in a solution of one part bleach to four parts water, allowing it to soak for 15 to 20 minutes. Rinse the doily completely, then starch it heavily and iron it flat. Any damaged areas on the outer edges can be carefully cut away with sharp scissors. To remove wax spots, which are common on doilies used beneath candlesticks, cover the blemishes with a few layers of paper towels and iron on low heat until the paper no longer absorbs any wax. Take your cleaned and ironed doilies to a professional framer to have them stitched onto matting, and frame them in simple frames—or use ready-made frames and acid-free mats. Avoid glue, because it may discolor the needlework. Choose a mat in a color that sets off the doily, keeping in mind that a darker color will provide more contrast. If you know the family history of your doilies, record it on the frame backing.

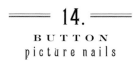

14.
BUTTON
picture nails

MATERIALS *LARGE BUTTON WITH SHANK, WIRE CUTTERS, EMERY BOARD, EPOXY, BUTTON COVER, SCREW OR HANGING NAIL, WIDE DECORATIVE RIBBON.* ⚜ When you pass a flea-market booth offering buttons by the can, stop and take a look, especially if you have small pictures to hang. **1.** Remove the shank with wire cutters, and smooth the back of the button with an emery board. Using epoxy, glue the button cover (available at fabric stores) to the back of the button. The back opening of the button cover, designed to slide over a plain button, fits as easily over a nail. **2.** Attach a screw or hanging nail to the wall, keeping in mind that the picture will hang several inches below it. Slide the button cover (and button) into place; snap closed. **3.** Thread ribbon through the eye hooks on the back of the frame, tie it in a double-knotted bow, and hang the picture, centering the bow above the button. To secure larger pieces, use picture wire in addition to ribbon.

LEFT: Beautiful, old-fashioned buttons can transform ordinary hardware and give an air reminiscent of nineteenth-century drawing rooms. **BELOW**: *Look for large buttons in Bakelite, bone, pressed glass, shell, or any other material that happens to catch your eye. Be sure they have wire loops (called shanks) rather than holes.*

N OT SO LONG AGO, THE DAILY ACTIVITIES OF COOKING, SERVING FOOD, AND WASHING UP REQUIRED NUMEROUS SPECIALIZED pieces of equipment no longer in use today. The paraphernalia that was necessary to run a proper Victorian household filled every corner of the house, but nowadays few people bake crackers at home, steam puddings, serve afternoon tea, or bathe in their bedrooms with a pitcher and basin. As those activities have become obsolete, so have the household objects associated with them, and a staggering number are available at flea markets all over the country. For every piece of furniture awaiting your perusal, there are likely to be dozens of utilitarian ceramics and kitchen items stacked on tables nearby.

⚜ Because it offers such a wealth of prospects for creative reuse, this is an excellent category for the beginning forager. Well-made, intrinsically beautiful objects that were once stored away in kitchen cabinets, pantry drawers, and washstands should be examined with an eye to their shapes and forms and possible reincarnation. Look for

Kitchenware & Ceramics

orphans of once intact sets, such as saucers without cups or basins that have lost their pitchers. Do not pass up a slightly chipped cup or a handsome platter broken neatly into two pieces. Such items are bargains that, with a little imagination, can be completely and grandly made over.

BRASS

This golden metal tarnishes to a deeper shade of gold and is usually spun or turned on a wheel rather than molded. For hundreds of years, brass has been used to make candlesticks, trays, doorknobs and knockers, and many other useful and decorative objects.

PEWTER

This silver-colored alloy contains tin and various other metals. Its lead content makes it heavy, and soft enough to bend with the force of a human hand. It was often used to make candlesticks and tableware from the seventeenth century through the 1950s. Unpolished pewter develops a dull patina, which many collectors prize.

ALUMINUM

Extremely light in both weight and color, aluminum resists rust and tarnish. It has been used since the early twentieth century to make everything from cooking pots to serving trays, as well as utensils. Nowadays the alloys are different, and few kitchenware pieces are made of pure aluminum.

STAINLESS STEEL

Like aluminum, stainless steel resists corrosion. Heavier and more durable than tin, it is used to make flatware, utensils, cooking pans, and the larger objects found in commercial kitchens, such as large baking sheets, countertops, tabletops, and sinks.

TIN

This metal is most often used to plate steel. Tin-plated objects are light and rust easily, and they often display seams from having been soldered together. Tin cookie cutters and bakeware were popular from the eighteenth century through the 1930s.

CAST IRON

In the nineteenth and early twentieth centuries, many cooking pots, pans, trivets, and flatirons were fashioned from this heavy, durable material. It takes its name from the casts, or molds, into which molten iron was poured, then allowed to cool. Its ability to conduct heat makes it a popular choice for cookware, especially skillets.

SILVER PLATE

Metal plated with a layer of silver is used to produce hollowware, flatware, and trays. Repeated polishing may wear away the plating, revealing the metal underneath. Invented in Sheffield, England, early silver plate used copper as a base and had no maker's mark. It has a softer glow than electroplate, which eventually replaced it.

COPPER

Softer and redder than brass, copper will turn green when exposed to air over a long period of time. Common copper pieces include pots, pans, teakettles, molds, and large serving vessels.

METAL: A CLEANING GUIDE

✦ Oven cleaner is excellent for resuscitating baking pans that are almost unrecognizable underneath years of baked-on grease. Spray pans thoroughly with the cleaner, then seal them in a heavy plastic bag for at least twenty-four hours. Wipe clean, and repeat the process if necessary. Oven cleaner also removes dirt and stains from enamel pieces like pots and basins.

✦ Brass, copper, pewter, and silver plate may be cleaned with commercial products formulated specifically for them.

✦ Plated items, such as silver saucers or tin pitchers, can be cleaned with very fine steel wool.

✦ Remove rust from tin or corrosion from aluminum by scrubbing with steel wool and naval jelly (available at hardware stores) or a commercial product such as Noxon.

✦ To clean a very dirty cast-iron skillet, first heat it in a 200-degree oven to loosen the grime. When it is cool enough to handle, pour a generous amount of salt into the pan, and scrub with a plastic scrubber or sponge. Discard the used salt, and then scrub again with new salt. Repeat until the salt remains fairly clean after scrubbing. Rinse the pan, and dry it thoroughly by holding it over a low burner or placing it upside down in a warm oven.

BUYING AND CARING FOR CERAMICS

The term *ceramic* refers to any object made of a nonmetallic mineral (such as clay) that has been fired and glazed at a high temperature. Most ceramic kitchenware is molded rather than shaped by hand. Porcelain, made of finer clay, is a thin, more translucent type of ceramic, often used to make fine tableware. It is almost always considerably more expensive than earthenware, although certainly not off-limits to bargain hunters. The following pointers will help you select and care for various types of ceramics commonly found at flea markets and tag sales:

✦ Tap a hollow vessel: If it rings like a bell, it should not have any cracks. Although a chip will not compromise a vessel's durability, a crack might do so, even if it is so small you can barely see it.

✦ If some of the gilding has flaked off a ceramic piece, you can remove the remainder with a pencil eraser or steel-wool soap pad. Remove paint by soaking the piece in ammonia.

✦ Glazed ceramics that are repeatedly exposed to intense heat, as from an oven, a dishwasher, or boiling water, may develop a superficial network of fine cracks called crazing. Avoid using them to serve food, which will catch in the cracks and stain the surface.

✦ Clean stained ceramics by simmering them in milk or soaking them in a denture-tablet solution.

✦ Don't use bleach on any ceramic. It will get under the glaze and begin to erode the ceramic material. If a white powdery substance reappears on a piece after washing, it has probably been bleached. Unfortunately, this damage is irreversible.

✦ To remove the mineral salts that often accumulate on ceramic planters, try using a commercial toilet-bowl cleanser.

✦ Don't submerge a ceramic vessel in hot water if it has been outside in the cold for a long time—as at a flea market in the fall. The sudden shift in temperature could cause it to crack or break.

Ceramics such as these white ironstone serving pieces should never be bleached; to clean, try soaking them in a denture-tablet solution instead.

WILLOW WARE

THE FAMILIAR WILLOW PATTERN WAS adapted in Western Europe in the eighteenth century from a motif found on Chinese porcelain. It tells a story of two separated lovers and their secret meeting in a garden with willow trees, a pagoda, and a bridge. Chinese wares began to appear in Western Europe in the seventeenth century, and as demand grew, so did the number of European manufacturers who copied the willow motif and other designs onto dishware. Faceup, these five plates may look similar, but the marks on the back tell very different stories. Learn to decipher the marks, and you will know whether you are looking at nineteenth-century British porcelain or earthenware mass-produced in Ohio in 1978.

early 19th century

To make transferware, a pattern is engraved on a copper plate, which is inked with porcelain glaze in blue, black, yellow, brown, green, or red. The pattern is then transferred to a sheet of tissue, which is pressed onto a plate. Early plates such as this English example often lack any marking on the back.

late 19th century

Any piece marked with just the name of the country of origin, as is this English ironstone transferware, was made between 1893 and 1905.

early 20th century

This piece of Japanese ironstone is marked "Flair" (the maker), "Japan" (country of origin), and "Blue Willow" (the pattern name).

The mark on this American earthenware plate, "Made in USA," dates it after 1910. According to the mark, the maker was Homer Laughlin.

mid 20th century

Marked "Made in England" and "Fine Myott Meakin Tableware," this plate exhibits a coarsening of detail, a sign of its relative modernity.

THE DIAMOND REGISTRY MARK

Between 1842 and 1883, English earthenware, such as ironstone and transferware, was marked with a highly specific dating system that indicated not only the year of manufacture but also the month and even the day. The key below will help you decipher those marks. Accompanying the maker's mark and the name of the pattern on the bottom of each piece, the diamonds are not always immediately apparent: Some were embossed rather than inscribed in ink, so look closely. If you are lucky, you will be able to say, for example, "This plate was made on November 18, 1862."

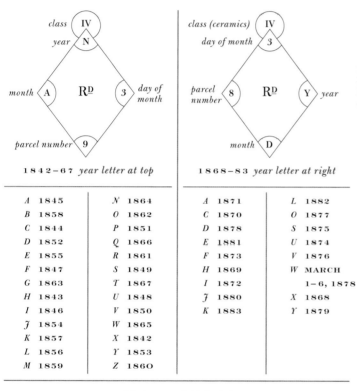

1842–67 *year letter at top*		1868–83 *year letter at right*	
A 1845	N 1864	A 1871	L 1882
B 1858	O 1862	C 1870	O 1877
C 1844	P 1851	D 1878	S 1875
D 1852	Q 1866	E 1881	U 1874
E 1855	R 1861	F 1873	V 1876
F 1847	S 1849	H 1869	W MARCH
G 1863	T 1867	I 1872	1–6, 1878
H 1843	U 1848	J 1880	X 1868
I 1846	V 1850	K 1883	Y 1879
J 1854	W 1865		
K 1857	X 1842		
L 1856	Y 1853		
M 1859	Z 1860		

MONTHS *both periods*

A	DECEMBER	K	NOVEMBER (AND
B	OCTOBER		DECEMBER 1860)
C or O	JANUARY	M	JUNE
D	SEPTEMBER	R	AUGUST (AND
E	MAY		SEPTEMBER
G	FEBRUARY		1–19, 1857)
H	APRIL	W	MARCH
I	JULY		

ABOVE: *Most mid-nineteenth-century English earthenware was stamped with the insignia of the company that made it (there were many), the pattern name (in this case, Yosemite), and the diamond registry mark, which tells you exactly when the piece was made.*

OPPOSITE: *Similar patterned tea-cups, each holding a potted minia-ture African violet, are clustered with stacks of cookies on cake stands for a charming display at a Mother's Day party. Guests are presented with the lovely favors as they head home.* **BELOW**: *A cup and saucer also work as a vase, to show off tiny short-stemmed cut flowers such as violets or lilies-of-the-valley.*

1.
TEACUP
cachepots and vases

IF YOU HAPPEN UPON A LONE TEACUP, CONSIDER FILLING it with something besides tea. Cups make fine individual cache-pots for small flowering plants. Keep the plants in their original plastic pots (complete with drainage holes), and slip one pot inside each cup. The plastic disappears, and the cup retains drained water and allows it to be reabsorbed. Flea-market tables abound with orphaned cups, both with and without saucers, so you will have no trouble finding inexpensive examples in a wide variety of colors. Match the floral pattern with the living bloom—violets with violets, say, or roses with miniature roses—or mix it up. March a line of teacup cachepots or vases down the middle of a dining table, or place a single one on a nightstand or front-hall shelf. For a more modern look, alternate solid-white ceramic or clear-glass examples with patterned ones. If you choose to use a teacup and saucer as a vase, you may want to set a flower frog in the bottom of the teacup to help hold cut blossoms in place.

OPPOSITE: *A collage of transfer-ware plates and platters evokes a nostalgic feeling.* ABOVE: *Simple patterns and solid-color plates, chosen for color and shape and arranged geometrically, provide a contemporary look. Vary the spaces separating the plates, and experiment with all sizes.* RIGHT: *To custom fit your plate hangers, you need a few simple tools and some 18-gauge annealed iron wire.*

MATERIALS *WIRE CUTTERS, 18-GAUGE ANNEALED IRON WIRE, PLATES, NEEDLE-NOSE PLIERS, WALL HOOKS.* ✄ For flea-market plates, it's a small leap from the table to the wall, where their contours make pleasing arrangements—the scale, patterns, and colors of many plates and platters are similar to those of framed watercolors and small prints. Make sure, however, that the hangers supporting them do not detract from their beauty. Unlike many store-bought hangers, the homemade ones shown here grip plates with even pressure and can safely accommodate any size or shape. Because it is soft and pliable, 18-gauge annealed iron wire can easily be manipulated to fit around a plate. **1.** Using wire cutters, cut two pieces of wire 3 inches longer than the diameter of your plate. Bend one piece into a V shape. **2.** Twist the second wire to make a loop in the center. This loop will be used to attach the hanger to a wall hook. Feed one end of the V-shaped wire through the loop; the V should be upside down, its crook resting on the bottom of the loop. Twist the V-shaped wire around itself once to secure. **3.** Position the wires on the back of the plate so the top of the loop hits the top edge of the plate base. Holding wires in position, wrap them tightly around the rim onto front of plate. **4.** Clip ends of wire to a uniform length. Using small needle-nose pliers, twist ends around to form decorative loops. A very large or heavy plate may need the support of one or two additional wires. **5.** Mark the proper placement on the wall, install wall hooks, and hang each plate.

OPPOSITE: *Aluminum baking pans and molds were made in many shapes and sizes. If you've updated to nonstick finishes, you can turn these tag-sale finds into atmospheric reflectors for candles.* LEFT: *Draw attention to the fanciful shapes of nineteenth-century tin and pewter dessert molds by displaying them on a tiered table, or create a wall display of ring and jelly molds.*

3.
DECORATIVE
molds

OLD-FASHIONED INTRICATE MOLDS MAY HAVE FALLEN OUT of style within the culinary world, but their decorative shapes and materials make them welcome additions in any room. Think like with like—copper with copper, for instance, or ironstone with ironstone—to make the strongest aesthetic statement. Many metal molds have a ring hook attached; for those that do not, use plate hangers (they come in adjustable sizes). You can also hang a ring mold from a ribbon passed through the center.

4.
BAKING PAN
sconces

MATERIALS *ALUMINUM BAKING PANS, TRAYS, OR MOLDS; ALUMINUM POLISH; PLATE HANGERS; NAILS; CANDLES; CLIP-ON CANDLE HOLDERS.* So that aluminum pans provide the proper reflective background, first bring them to a bright shine with a commercial aluminum polish. Mount pans on the wall before you attach the candle holders and insert candles. Inexpensive clip-on holders with fluted rims to catch excess wax are available at Christmas specialty stores. To hang the sconces, use plate hangers or simply hammer a nail through the pan into the wall. Narrow, circular, or polygonal pans or trays require only one candle; wider pans look best with two or three. Center a single holder, but space multiple holders evenly across one edge of pans.

RIGHT: *Clean, paint, or otherwise spruce up the outside of a bread box before putting it to use as a silver chest. We used white nail polish to touch up the chips in this enameled box.* BELOW: *Lay the silver on a tarnish-resistant fabric pillow, and surround it with more of the same fabric to help keep it unscratched and shiny.*

5.
BREAD BOX
silver chest

MATERIALS *SEWING SCISSORS, METAL BREAD BOX, FABRIC, FABRIC PENCIL, BATTING.* **1.** Cut a piece of soft, durable fabric eight to ten times as large as the interior surface area of your bread box. **2.** To make the cushion, place the box very close to one corner of the fabric, and trace its outline with the fabric pencil; ½ inch outside the line, make a parallel dotted line. **3.** Cut out the piece along the dotted line, then cut an identical piece. **4.** Stack the pieces right sides together, pin, then sew a ½-inch seam, leaving a small opening at one of the short ends. Trim seams and cut curves at corners. Turn right side out, fill with batting, and sew shut. **5.** To complete the lining, cut remaining fabric into two strips—one the same length as the box and three times as wide, the other as wide as the box and three times as long (see diagram at left). **6.** Place the cushion in the box, and arrange the fabric strips on top. Add silverware, and fold fabric flaps over it to cover before closing the lid.

TEACUPS WITHOUT HANDLES WERE COMMON UNTIL THE LATE NINETEENTH CENTURY, and a solitary surviving cup and saucer from a set will often turn up at a flea market. You can create a pretty and useful serving compote by upending the cup and placing the saucer on top. It is best to match materials (porcelain with porcelain) and to consider scale (a tiny saucer would not look right on a tall cup), but colors and patterns may be mixed at will. Wash and dry both pieces thoroughly before you begin. Roll eight to ten ¼-inch balls of soft wax or adhesive putty, then place them evenly around the base of the upturned cup. Center the saucer, and press it firmly into the wax. This joint is not permanent, so expect the pieces to separate during washing.

MATERIALS *CERAMIC PLATTER, MEASURING TAPE, PAPER, MIRROR, PILLOW PIPING, CRAFT GLUE, PAINTBRUSH, CERAMIC EPOXY OR MOUNTING TAPE, PLATE HANGER.* **1.** Select a plate or platter whose border pattern is mostly intact. With a measuring tape, measure the perimeter of the platter's central well at its flattest edge. Measure each side, since old ceramics are not always perfectly symmetrical. **2.** Draw the measured shape on a piece of paper, then cut it out to make a template. Check for accuracy by laying the template on the platter. It should fit and lie flat. **3.** If you are using a round plate, you may be able to purchase a circular mirror of the right size at a crafts store. Otherwise, have a professional glass cutter custom-cut a mirror from your template. Request a polished edge, which is prettier and safer to handle. **4.** For braided trim around the glass, as pictured at left, attach pillow piping. Cut the piping 1 inch longer than the perimeter of the mirror. Starting a few inches from one end, dab craft glue with a fine paintbrush onto a few inches of the flat side of the piping, and then press piping onto the mirror's edge (see photograph at bottom left). Hold this piece in place while it dries, and then continue applying glue to the rest of the piping in 1-inch segments and pressing it onto the mirror's edge. When the piping is almost completely in place but before you've reached the point where the two ends meet, trim the excess. To prevent fraying, singe both ends of the piping with a match, and glue them together. Tuck any stray threads into the glue, and glue the last section of piping to the mirror. **5.** To attach the mirror to the platter permanently, apply ceramic epoxy to the back of the mirror in a big X from side to side and in a thin line just within the perimeter. Press the mirror onto the platter. The epoxy must be dry before you hang the finished mirror. If you would like to be able to remove the mirror in the future, use mounting tape instead of glue. Peel off one side of the tape backing, and affix a grid of tape to the back of the mirror. Peel off the other side of the backing, and press the mirror onto the platter. **6.** To mount the platter mirror on the wall, use a plate hanger of the appropriate size.

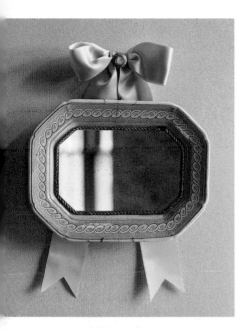

Vintage plates or platters—even scratched, cracked, or broken ones—make beautiful frames for mirrors. **OPPOSITE:** *This platter was transformed into a decorative bathroom mirror.* **THIS PAGE:** *The broken pieces of this platter (below left) were rejoined with epoxy. Once the mirror is in place, the repair is barely noticeable.*

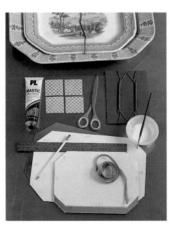

BOTTOM: *Even houseplants in plain clay pots can look dressed up. Set them atop silver saucers or trays, and they will leave no rings or traces of soil on a tabletop.* **BELOW**: *Inexpensive finds include silver-plated coasters, trivets, and trophy plates. Worn plating or somebody else's monogram will end up hidden underneath the pot. Edges will remain visible, however, so look for those with decorative patterns.*

8.

SILVER
pot saucers

MATERIALS *SILVER OR SILVER-PLATED SAUCERS OR TRAYS, CLOTHS, DISHWASHING DETERGENT, SILVER POLISH, SELF-ADHESIVE FELT SURFACE PROTECTORS, POTTED PLANTS.* Once you have obtained a few nice silver saucers or small trays to support your houseplants, take the time to make their surfaces gleam. Wash each piece by hand with a soft cloth dampened in a solution of warm water and a few drops of mild dishwashing detergent (do not soak silver plate). Washing removes harmful chemicals before they can tarnish the surface of the silver. Dry thoroughly with another soft cloth. Polish the saucers with a mild commercial polish specifically formulated for silver. In general, polish-imbued cloths and liquid polishes are sufficient for light tarnish, whereas surfaces that have turned almost black from the passage of time and exposure to air require a paste or cream. Follow the manufacturer's instructions carefully. You may need to polish a severely tarnished piece several times. Wash and dry the piece. Press four self-adhesive felt surface protectors (available at housewares stores) onto the base of each saucer or tray. These will not only save your furniture from scratches but also help prevent the saucer or tray from slipping.

= 9. =

HANGING
bird basin

MATERIALS *WIRE CUTTERS, 18-GAUGE COPPER WIRE, WASH BASIN WITH A WIDE LIP, MEASURING TAPE, LEAD SLEEVES, NEEDLE-NOSE PLIERS, HOOK, STONE (FOR PERCH).* Cut a length of copper wire 4 inches longer than the circumference of the bowl just below the lip. Thread 2 inches of wire through a lead sleeve; loop wire around and through the sleeve a second time. Pinch with needle-nose pliers to secure. From the other end, thread eight sleeves onto this ring wire, spacing them evenly in pairs. Secure each sleeve by pinching it with pliers to close around wire. Cut four pieces of wire to desired hanging length; loop one end of each between each pair of sleeves. Slip a new sleeve onto each hanging wire, and secure the loop (see bottom photo, right). Thread one more sleeve onto ring wire. Form ring wire into a circle, looping one end through the original loop, then threading it through the last sleeve and securing it. Insert basin. Twist hanging wires together several inches from top, and form a knot, using pliers. Hang from a hook.

TOP: *Ironstone basins that have lost their pitchers are among the better bargains at flea markets and tag sales.* **LEFT**: *Often they are so inexpensive that you won't mind sharing one with feathered friends.* **ABOVE**: *Our bird-basin project requires only copper wire, a pair of pliers, and a few lead sleeves, but adding a rock to the basin will help smaller birds wade or drink.*

10.
CERAMIC
organizers

MID-TWENTIETH-CENTURY FLORISTS COMMONLY USED ceramic planters to hold growing greenery. Whether unmarked or stamped with a well-known name, such as McCoy, Roseville, or Frankoma, they make handy repositories for any number of household items today. Use a color-coordinated group to organize a tea tray (opposite) or to house bathroom essentials (above). Similarly, chipped white pudding and pâté molds can provide a home for cotton balls, swabs, and facecloths (left). To clean vintage pottery, a thorough washing by hand with soap and water should suffice; for tougher stains, try a mildly abrasive cleansing powder such as Bon Ami first, and then work your way up to very fine steel wool, taking care not to scratch the glaze.

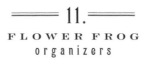

AT FLEA MARKETS AND TAG SALES, FLORAL FROGS USUALLY TURN UP IN ONE OF TWO traditional forms: a smooth, rounded shape made of a waterproof material such as bronze, lead, glass, or pottery, pierced with regular holes (below left), or a metal kenzan, or needle mountain, invented by the Japanese (below right). The stem holes in a ceramic frog are the right size for holding pens, pencils, paintbrushes, or toothbrushes. A needle mountain that no longer impales sturdy flower stems is helpful in straightening desktop clutter or holding recipe cards on a kitchen counter.

BELOW: *Long a fixture of floral design, decorative frogs have yielded to more utilitarian-looking examples or to floral foam.* **RIGHT**: *Release a flower frog or needle mountain from its traditional task—stabilizing flower stems at the bottom of a vase—and you will discover that it does a fine job of organizing odds and ends at home or in the office.*

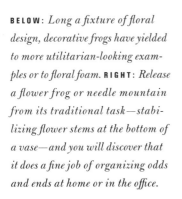

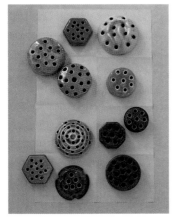

BELOW: *These sturdy, streamlined examples of the porcelain-coated metal known as enamelware are plentiful at secondhand sales. Shallow trays once accommodated dental tools; deeper boxes kept refrigerated food fresh in the days before plastic.* **LEFT**: *Use an assortment of shapes and sizes to hold papers and other office supplies. To add to a unified ensemble, transform a tray into a bulletin board.*

12.
ENAMELWARE
organizers

MANY OTHERWISE NICE ENAMELWARE TRAYS AND BOXES ARE PASSED OVER AT FLEA markets because they are chipped or stained. This needn't stop you from taking one home. Clean trays and boxes thoroughly by washing them in a solution of dishwashing liquid and water. For tougher stains, soak the enamelware in a solution of 1 tablespoon bleach to 1 quart warm water. If a piece is chipped, repair the damage by applying a few coats of nail polish in a matching shade (right). You may need to take your enamelware piece to the beauty-supply store so that you can match the paint colors. Apply several coats of nail polish, building up the patched surface until it is level with the enamel. To make an enamelware bulletin board, mount a tray on the wall using a platter hanger, then use magnets instead of tacks to hold everything in place.

THE HARDWARE AND ARCHITECTURAL COMPONENTS OF PAST ERAS ARE GENERALLY OF FINER QUALITY THAN ALL BUT THEIR most expensive modern counterparts, yet many can be bought at bargain prices. Think of wooden trim adorned with crisply cut acanthus leaves and acorns, or the sleek lines of industrial metalwork from the 1920s and '30s. Many of the utilitarian bits and pieces from the nineteenth and twentieth centuries were made in pleasing shapes from high-quality materials such as heavy chrome, sleek enamel, and solid hardwood. Today, constant renovation or razing of old buildings ensures a steady supply at salvage yards and flea markets of windows, doors, hooks, knobs, plumbing and light fixtures, mantels, cornices, and other architectural details. Each of these objects presents a wide range of possibilities. You might choose to flank your win-

dows with vintage shutters or hang coats on antique hooks, but you do not have to stop there. Surround a mirror with a window frame of weathered wood, use cut-glass doorknobs from

Hardware & Salvage

the thirties as towel hooks, or fill the negative space in a displaced mantel with upholstered plywood to create a headboard. A set of brass drawer pulls can transform a bureau or a roomful of window shades. You don't have to be a master carpenter to make use of most salvage finds; an appreciation of their inherent beauty is what counts.

ASSESSING A FIND

It's important to know exactly what kind of material you are dealing with before you try to clean, strip, paint, or refinish a find. Enamel, brass, marble, glass, iron, plastic, or any other material needs to be handled in specific ways with specific products. However, when an item is covered with several coats of paint or years of tarnish, it can be difficult to assess. Ask a salvage-yard proprietor or flea-market merchant what something is made of before you buy it. Try the magnet test to determine if a metal is solid brass or copper (a magnet won't attach itself to either) rather than plated steel. Check to see if a wooden piece is solid, laminated, or veneered: If the grain is very different on the top and sides, it is probably solid; very similar, and it's likely to be veneered. Examine a cutting board for practice.

BRINGING AN OUTSIDE PIECE INDOORS

Any object that has spent considerable time outdoors may have become infested with pests. To avoid bringing unwanted visitors into the house, run water through hollow tubing on metal pieces such as bed frames or table legs. If you notice suspicious repetitive holes in a wooden piece, place a sheet of black paper underneath it and leave it outdoors but well covered. Within a week, if you see fresh sawdust on the paper, the wood is probably infested with termites. To prevent further damage to a small item, wrap it in a sealable plastic freezer bag and place it in the freezer for several weeks (cold will kill insects and larvae). Place a larger item in a garbage bag and set off an insect bomb inside it (never do this indoors), then immediately seal the bag. A bug exterminating spray might also work, depending on the extent of the infestation.

PRESERVING PATINA

Unlike materials carefully stored indoors, such as fabric, ceramics, and glass, most vintage hardware and architectural salvage shows the effects of exposure to the elements and the passage of time. Copper objects turn a soft metallic green. Brass, bronze, and other metals take on a deep, burnished appearance. Wood weathers, becoming softer and grayer. Painted surfaces chip or flake, revealing areas of the material underneath, often in an attractive pattern. These changes may be well worth preserving. Think carefully before you decide to strip or paint an object that is showing its age. The look can be charming, and once the patina is gone, it will take another lifetime to achieve.

CLEANING AND STRIPPING

Of course, not all pieces of hardware and salvage show their age so gracefully. Some are covered in dull radiator paint or cloudy varnish; others are so grimy that it is impossible to tell what covers them. Beautifully carved or molded detail may have all but disappeared under layers of paint. For those objects, you will want to uncover the original surfaces. Here are some guidelines:

BRASS: Remove tarnish with a commercial product specifically formulated for brass. Never use acids, such as lemon juice, vinegar, or ammonia, or commercial glass cleaners. A coat of paste wax, applied after polishing, will retard tarnish.

CAST IRON: Because this material is porous and absorbs water, it tends to rust; pieces that have become wet should be thoroughly dry before you seal or paint them. Remove small rust spots with a utility knife; strip larger areas with steel wool.

CHROME: Used to plate other metals, chrome does not tarnish, although the underlying metal may, causing pockmarks. If you try to scrape off such marks, the corrosion will worsen. For an

RIGHT: *The paint on this wooden table has mellowed to a beautiful finish that is worth preserving. It would be a shame to hide the well-earned patina under a coat of shiny new paint.* **OPPOSITE**: *Liz's Antique Hardware in Los Angeles is renowned for its vast selection of antique hardware. Owner Liz Gordon carries more than a half-million vintage and contemporary pieces for doors, windows, curtains, lamps, furniture, and baths.*

has lost its shine, apply lacquer thinner, available at paint stores.

STAINLESS STEEL: Any spots may be removed with a cleaner formulated specifically for this material, such as Noxon. Polish in straight motions, following the grain of the metal.

TIN: Clean tin or tinplate with a soft cloth and soapy water, then put it in a 200-degree oven to dry thoroughly (any moisture trapped in seams can quickly rust the metal).

WOOD, PAINTED: Painted wood can be wiped or patted clean, depending on the surface. If the piece has brittle, peeling layers, scrape it with a table knife or single-edge razor blade. Remove remaining paint with a commercial stripper, available at hardware stores. Work in a well-ventilated area, and follow the manufacturer's instructions. Acetone may be used to remove gilding.

WOOD, UNPAINTED: Apply a household cleaning product such as Spic 'n' Span or Soilex, available at paint and hardware stores, with a soft sponge or rag to remove grease or residue. If tough stains persist, try using steel wool and water.

WOOD, VARNISHED: Remove old varnish by applying denatured alcohol, available at paint and hardware stores.

PAINTING, FINISHING, AND AGING METAL

PAINTING: Clean all metal surfaces thoroughly before applying a primer designed specifically for metal. Top the primer coat with an oil-based spray paint, available at hardware stores.

FINISHING: Once a metal piece has been cleaned and all tarnish and rust have been removed, you can seal the newly pristine finish by applying a clear coat of spray-on lacquer—or you can polish the object at intervals to keep tarnish at bay. Although a lacquered surface requires less maintenance, the lacquer is likely to break down over time, causing the metal to tarnish unevenly. When this happens, the lacquer should be stripped.

AGING: Most vintage hardware has lost its original nuts, bolts, or screws. Make sure any new mounting hardware you choose is appropriate to your vintage piece in size, color, and material. This makes all the difference between a cohesive effect and a hodgepodge. You can give hardware the patina of age by simply leaving it outside, exposed to the elements. If the object is copper or brass, place it next to an open container of ammonia inside a

even shine, buff water spots with a soft cotton cloth. Clean any discoloration with commercial chrome cleaner.

ENAMEL: Enamel is a coating made of small glass particles, which is baked onto cast iron or other metals. It is usually found on kitchenware, medical supplies, and industrial parts. Because the surface is nonporous, enamel is easier to clean and maintain than raw metal surfaces susceptible to rust. Clean dirty or stained enamel with an oven cleaner or a household scrubbing agent such as Soft Scrub. Small pieces can be touched up with nail polish.

GILT BRONZE: To remove paint, stains, and tarnish from a particular item, use acetone, available at hardware stores.

LACQUERED METAL: Lacquer is commonly used as a sealant to prevent tarnish on brass or copper household pieces and door knockers, knobs, and plates. To remove lacquer that is peeling or

clear plastic bag for several minutes or hours, depending on how dark you want it to be. Since this change happens rapidly and unevenly, keep careful watch, and extract the piece as soon as it starts to discolor. If it acquires too much patina, use fine steel wool to return it to its original condition, then try again. Repeat the process until you have reached the desired finish.

THE EVOLUTION OF HOOKS

Like other examples of architectural hardware, the simple utilitarian wall hook has evolved over centuries. The timeline at right offers a guide to determining the era in which a particular hook was produced. Handwrought hooks from the late eighteenth and early nineteenth centuries reflect the preindustrial society of early America and echo the classical lines of its architecture. Before the Victorian era, household closets were rare (since most people didn't have an abundance of clothing to put in them). Most wardrobes and those early closets that did exist had hooks rather than bars. Some mid-nineteenth-century hooks were handmade, but many exemplified the mass production that prevailed later in the century. In the decades after the Civil War, hooks became as varied as American society—from the simple wrought-iron examples still used on Midwestern farms to the ornate extravaganzas made for urban vestibules. By the twentieth century, closets had become far more common, and hooks were largely relegated to the bathroom and mudroom. At the same time, most hooks were being mass-produced out of newer rust-resistant materials such as aluminum, stainless steel, and chrome.

LATE 18TH TO EARLY 19TH CENTURY: In the Colonial and Federal periods, nails were made by hand and therefore precious, and were often recycled as hooks—like the three rosehead hand-forged nails pictured at the top of the column. Later, hooks were purpose-made of hand-turned brass or forged cast iron. The hook pictured third from the bottom is typical of the earliest square-cut machine-made nails.

19TH CENTURY: Hooks in attractive shapes with porcelain heads and embossed patterns were cast and molded by machine. A relief pattern covers the entire surface of the large cast-iron hook second from the top. Fourth from the top is a picture hook from 1860.

LATE 19TH TO EARLY 20TH CENTURY: Hooks were mass-produced in a wider range of materials, including brass, bronze, iron, glass, nickel, and steel. Shapes echo contemporary furniture styles, from period revivals to Arts and Crafts. The top hook, with a pressed-glass head, and the fifth from the top, with two porcelain knobs, represent popular forms at the turn of the twentieth century. The third hook from the bottom embodies the bold simplicity favored by Arts and Crafts designers.

20TH CENTURY: Like Modernist architecture and furniture, hooks took inspiration from the sleek shapes of industrial design. Chrome plating was often the finish of choice, to reflect this Machine Age aesthetic. Streamlined Art Deco fixtures, such as the second hook from the top in the fourth column, evoked the glamour of cars, airplanes, and other contemporary marvels.

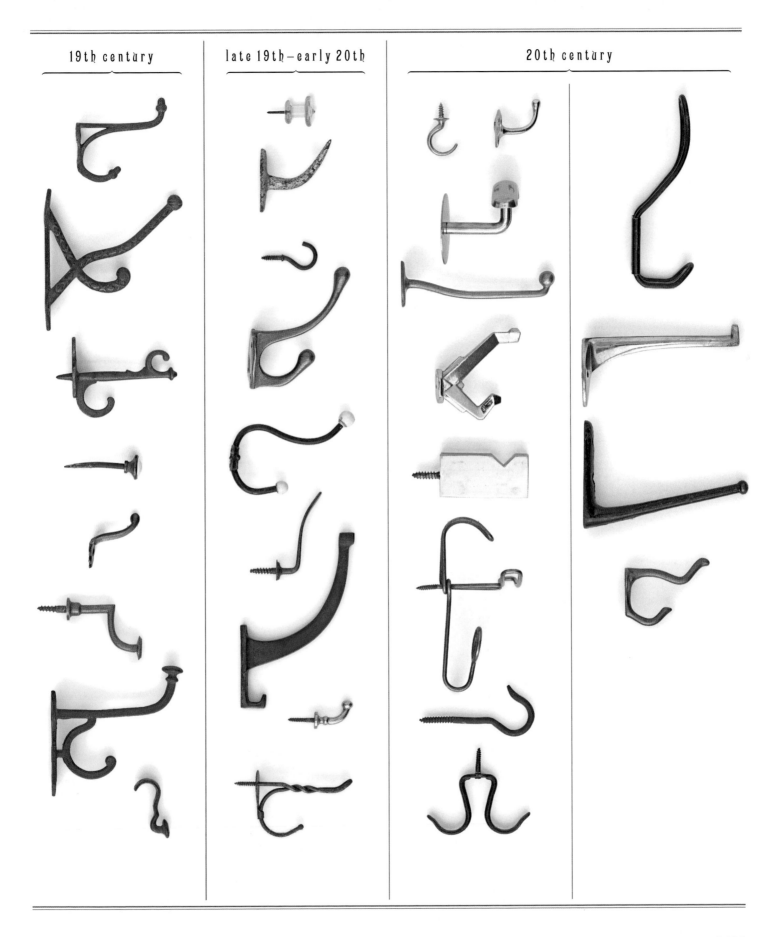

1.
HARDWARE
accessories

THE DRAWER PULLS AND COAT HOOKS MADE IN THE LATE nineteenth century are sturdy and often quite decorative. Many, like the examples shown below and at right, are cast brass, which was often gilded or painted, in the eclectic style of the Aesthetic Movement. Look for them at salvage yards and flea markets. Mount drawer pulls on roller blinds to add practical yet decorative detail. Use ½-inch screws to attach the pull, cup side down, to the wooden strip inside the bottom of the blind. Since the patina of old metal pulls and hooks can clash with shiny new screws, you may wish to darken the screws to match. Place brass or steel screws next to a dish of ammonia inside an airtight plastic bag. In about 15 minutes, the fumes will have tarnished the metal. Remove screws as soon as they have achieved the desired finish. Another quick fix: Use a permanent marker to color screw heads. If the pull or hook has been painted white, use correction fluid or white nail polish on new screws.

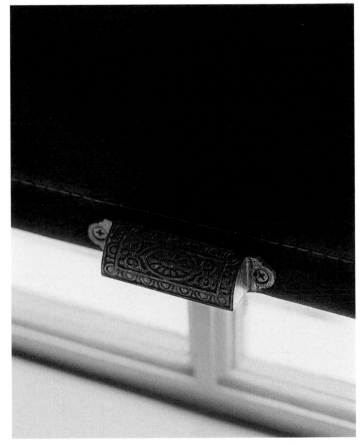

ABOVE: *A cast-brass drawer pull does handsome duty on a window shade.* **LEFT AND OPPOSITE**: *Vintage metal coat hooks were once mundane objects, but their graceful designs are much more distinctive than plain modern examples. Unearth a set from a box at a junk shop, and use them to hang coats or bathrobes or to embellish simple trim, as do these hooks attached to a hallway picture rail.*

2.

MANTELSHELF
console

MATERIALS *MARBLE MANTEL, WOODEN BRACKETS, LEVEL, DRILL, SIX TOGGLE BOLTS AT LEAST 3 INCHES LONG WITH BUTTERFLIES (FOR DRYWALL), SCREWS, SCREWDRIVER, LAG BOLTS WITH LEAD ANCHORS (FOR BRICK OR MASONRY WALL), WOOD GLUE, PLYWOOD UNDERSHELF, SILICONE (OPTIONAL).* Because marble is very heavy, properly anchored brackets are crucial to a secure wall mount. If you are not sure you can install a mantelshelf properly, consult a professional carpenter. Construct an undershelf of ½-inch plywood, cut to fit just shy of the contour of the marble. **1.** Measure and mark the desired height of the shelf. Also mark the screw holes for attaching brackets. Use a level so mantel and brackets will meet cleanly and sit level. **2.** For drywall: With a drill bit gauged for a toggle bolt, drill the three holes you marked in the wall for one bracket. Unscrew butterflies from three toggle bolts; thread screws through the holes in the brackets, and screw the butterflies onto the other side. Hold the bracket up to drilled holes; push butterflies through until they spring open on other side of wall. Tighten the screws until the brackets are flush against the wall. For masonry wall: Use a tungsten bit to drill three lead-anchor-size holes in the wall for a lag bolt. Insert an anchor in each hole; the fit should be tight. If the wall is brick, bore every hole through a brick, not through a mortar joint, which could crumble. **3.** Repeat step 2 with second bracket. **4.** If brackets come with wooden plugs (for concealing bolt heads), affix them with wood glue. **5.** Attach plywood undershelf to brackets with screws. **6.** Set marble atop plywood; the weight of the stone will hold it in place, but for maximum stability, join marble to the plywood with a layer of silicone.

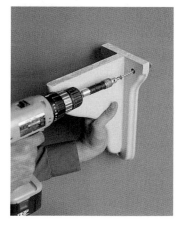

ABOVE: *Use a discarded marble mantelshelf to build bracketed consoles for your favorite possessions. A new stone slab would be expensive to cut and install, but you can find well-carved vintage ones at salvage yards for reasonable prices.* **OPPOSITE**: *In a variation of the traditional mantel over a fireplace, these shelves can be mounted one above another for an even more dramatic display.*

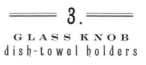

3.
GLASS KNOB
dish-towel holders

EVERY KITCHEN NEEDS PLENTY OF DISH TOWELS, AND A ROW OF VINTAGE GLASS KNOBS is a pretty way to keep them organized and handy. The knobs shown here date from the mid-nineteenth to the mid-twentieth century. The smaller knobs were probably used on kitchen and medicine cabinets, the larger ones attached to dresser drawers. It can be difficult to find a complete set of vintage knobs (unless you remove them from an old dresser), but a mixture of sizes, shapes, and patterns of cut glass can look charming. Vintage knobs at flea markets and salvage yards usually cost anywhere from $5 to $35 each, depending on their condition and age. To mount them in the kitchen, pick an area where the knobs will be visible and convenient for hanging dish towels. Attach knobs to the wall with screws at least 3 inches long. This will prevent them from loosening. The screws should fit snugly and be tightened flush against the fronts of the knobs.

ABOVE: *Although their rods are long gone, enameled, ceramic, and metal towel-bar supports from the thirties and forties often turn up at flea markets and salvage yards. Their appealing heft and shape call for new uses.* **TOP**: *Coordinate an enamel pair with the kitchen's color scheme, and use them with a copper rod to hold pots and pans.* **LEFT**: *A chrome-plated pair supports a bedroom curtain rod.*

═══ 4. ═══
TOWEL-BAR HOLDER
pot rack and curtain rod

MATERIALS *TOWEL-BAR HOLDERS, TOGGLE BOLTS (FOR DRY-WALL), LAG BOLTS WITH LEAD ANCHORS (FOR BRICK OR MASONRY WALLS), DRYWALL SCREWS (FOR CURTAIN ROD), SCREWDRIVER, COPPER PIPE AND S-HOOKS (FOR RACK), METAL GALVANIZED PIPE OR WOODEN DOWEL (FOR CURTAIN ROD), MODEL PAINT, SMALL PAINTBRUSH (OPTIONAL).* For a kitchen rack, the copper pipe needs to be sturdy enough to support heavy pots and pans. For stability, it should be no more than 4 feet long. (You can have it cut at a hardware store for a nominal fee.) Hardware openings should be only slightly wider than the diameter of the pipe they will be supporting; pipe diameters vary from ½ inch to 1¼ inches. **1.** Measure and mark the desired height of the bar, then measure and mark the placement of the hardware for one end. **2.** If you have drywall, use toggle bolts. For brick or other masonry walls, use lag bolts with lead anchors. Consult your hardware store concerning the proper bolts for your walls. For curtain rods, drywall screws will suffice, unless your curtains are very heavy. Attach toggle or lag bolts, and screw in one piece of towel-bar hardware. **3.** Insert pipe or dowel securely into opening. Because pipes or dowels can't be easily removed once installed, curtains should have tab tops or button or Velcro closures so they can be taken down for cleaning. **4.** Insert pipe or dowel securely into second piece of hardware, and slide it into place. **5.** Repeat steps 1 and 2 with pipe or dowel in place. If desired, use model paint and a small brush to cover the heads of the screws or bolts on hardware to match after mounting.

MATERIALS *CHEST, WOODEN BLOCKS, WOOD GLUE, MATCH-
ING DOORKNOBS WITH PLATES, ¼-INCH WOODEN DOWELS,
DRILL, SCREWS, SCREWDRIVER.* ❧ **1.** For the chest opposite,
glue four 1-by-1-by-2-inch blocks into the bottom inside corners
of the chest to hold the screws when the doorknobs are attached
to the chest. Let glue dry. **2.** Remove spindles from doorknobs
by taking out the setscrew in each shank. Cut five 2½-inch-long
wooden dowels. Apply glue to dowels, and insert each into a
knob. Replace setscrews. Invert chest, and place doorknob plates
over corners. With a pencil, mark screw holes and large hole in
the center of the plate. Use ¼-inch bit to drill center holes. For
doorknob plates, predrill holes using a ⁷⁄₆₄-inch bit; attach with
wood screws. Coat dowels with glue; insert them into large
holes. **3.** Turn chest over to attach handle. Glue a wood block to
the inside center of lid, let dry. Attach doorknob to lid as the feet
were attached but without the plate. To give feet to a jewelry box,
below, predrill holes using a ⁷⁄₆₄-inch bit, and screw drawer pulls
into place. For the handle, use a drawer-pull bolt and nut (available at hardware stores) instead of a screw.

OPPOSITE: *Smooth vintage doorknobs give a boxy blanket chest a
decorative lift and help it slide
across the rug when it's time to vac-
uum. A complementary doorknob
handle completes the transformation. Metal and ceramic doorknobs
(with plates) are sold in pairs at
flea markets, so you will have to
match only two sets. Glass knobs
won't support heavy chests but can
serve as handles.* **RIGHT**: *To create
a miniature footed chest, attach
drawer pulls to the base and front
of a wooden jewelry box.*

OPPOSITE AND BELOW: *Sets of metal label frames from old file cabinets, along with vintage window lifts, can be polished and reborn as picture hooks.* **LEFT AND ABOVE:** *Look for metal baskets of different sizes in a variety of configurations, from punched holes to a wire grid; then line them with natural-colored canvas and group them on shelves and floor to organize an entire roomful of clutter.*

6.
WIRE BASKET
storage bins

MATERIALS *VINTAGE METAL BASKET, NATURAL-COLORED CANVAS, NATURAL-COLORED TWILL TAPE, SEWING MACHINE.* Metal baskets once used to haul milk bottles or deliver groceries make perfect storage units for the kitchen or office—particularly when simply lined with canvas. **1.** Select two pieces of canvas—one large enough to cover the length of the basket including the bottom and short sides, and the other to cover the width and longer sides. Leave generous seam allowances on all sides. Hem the bottom (wider) section of the lining on either end. **2.** Create a ¾-inch open channel on the long sides. **3.** Hem the sides of the top (narrower) piece of canvas, then create the ¾-inch open channels at both ends. **4.** Lay top piece over bottom piece, and sew them together where they overlap, ½ inch in from the intersection on the longer sides and ¾ inch in from the intersection on the shorter sides. **5.** Cut four lengths of twill tape, each the length of the top of one side of the basket, plus 4 inches. Run twill tape through channels, leaving ends dangling. **6.** Place completed lining in basket, and secure it by tying twill tape pieces to the basket and each other, at each corner.

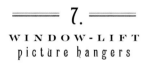

7.
WINDOW-LIFT
picture hangers

YOU CAN TAKE HOME A GENEROUS HANDFUL OF VINTAGE brass and nickel window lifts or label frames from your local salvage yard for between $3 and $5 each. For hanging pictures, shine the lifts with a polish formulated specifically for the metal of choice, fit them out with matching screws, and mount them on the wall upside down (opposite to the position they take on a window). Mid-twentieth-century window lifts are the perfect shape to support the hanging wires of a collection of flea-market prints or photographs in vintage frames, and their clean lines and metallic finish add a crisp design element to any arrangement.

INVITE A FEW OF THE SHAPELY GARDEN URNS AT YOUR LOCAL SALVAGE YARD TO COME indoors for the winter and sit cozily by the fire until spring arrives. Fat classical urns like these are the perfect size for holding firewood, rolls of newspaper and other kindling, or pinecones. For an air of formality, you might want to flank the firebox with a matched pair. A trio of mixed shapes and sizes clustered off to one side makes a more casual hearth. These examples of marble and cast cement date from the first half of the twentieth century. If an urn has spent any time outside, it will have developed a rich, mossy patina, which you will want to preserve. Instead of scrubbing it, gently remove any loose dirt and debris using a bottle brush. Rinse the inside of the urn with water (don't use soap, which could damage whatever plant you might want to put in it, come springtime). Attach felt pads to the bottoms of the urns so they won't scratch the floor.

BELOW: *Garden urns were once found in every suburban and country garden, where they were used to decorate outdoor living spaces and punctuate green vistas. Their enduring popularity makes them a common site at flea markets and salvage yards.* **RIGHT**: *If you spot an attractive example, bring it indoors, where it can become a decorative element in your living room.*

9.
STAMP RACK AND LAMP STAND
candleholders

OFFICE DESKS WERE ONCE EQUIPPED WITH STAINLESS- steel stands to hold old-fashioned hand stamps reading "Paid," "Expired," or "Overdue." Rendered obsolete by the computer age, these well-shaped holders now turn up at flea markets and modest antiques shops, carrying temptingly small price tags. Their adjustable clamps make them good candleholders (above). Place your stand atop a stainless-steel or silver-plated tray to elevate it from its industrial origins and catch drips of wax. For thicker candles, check the same vintage sources for cast-iron wall-mounted stands that were designed to hold oil lamps (right). These fixtures were made in two pieces—the swiveling arm that held the lamp (allowing you to pull it toward you to light it or blow it out) and the matching bracket that mounts on the wall. The former attaches to the latter with a vertical peg. Be sure that all the parts are included before you purchase the fixture.

Lightbulbs replaced candles in chandeliers for practicality's sake. Why shouldn't candles replace bulbs in old sockets, for the sake of romance? **BELOW**: *Early twentieth-century porcelain ceiling and wall fixtures in pleasant, neutral colors—and excellent condition—can be found for a few dollars a box at a salvage yard.* **RIGHT**: *Nestled in saucers, they make pretty candlesticks; smaller sockets look good holding votive candles. Remove any wax that collects in the sockets by placing the piece in the freezer; after a few minutes, the wax will contract and come loose.*

10.
LIGHT FIXTURE
candlesticks

MATERIALS *PORCELAIN BULB SOCKETS, WIRE CUTTERS, SCREWDRIVER, SINGLE-EDGE RAZOR BLADE OR PAINT STRIPPER, SAUCERS.* **1.** You'll find that many old porcelain light fixtures still have aging wires and electrical innards attached. Use wire cutters and a screwdriver to disconnect and extract all wiring and other electrical fittings. (If you decide to reuse the fixture for an electric light, insert new fittings that meet modern standards.) Remove the pull cord or chain, all screws, and anything else made of metal. Scrape any dried paint off the porcelain with a razor blade or paint stripper, following the manufacturer's instructions. **2.** Wash the fixture in warm, soapy water; rinse and dry. Set the fixture on a saucer that is wide enough to catch drips as the candle melts. Heat the bottom of a candle until it melts slightly, or drip some hot wax into the socket hole. Position the candle in the center, and hold it for a few seconds until the wax dries and anchors it.

11.
SOAP DISH
shelves

A SOAP DISH LIBERATED FROM THE BATHROOM IS THE RIGHT SIZE AND SHAPE TO HOLD small household odds and ends. Two vintage porcelain soap dishes mounted beneath an entryway mirror (below) organize keys, stamps, and loose change—necessities that are otherwise easily misplaced or forgotten. A soap dish above a bedroom bureau might hold rings and earrings; hang one beside a fireplace to hold matches. The soap dishes pictured at right date from the early to middle twentieth century and range in price from about $5 to $35 at flea markets and tag sales. Vintage chrome and glass examples are more expensive than those made of porcelain. Don't forgo a metal soap dish because it looks too dirty or corroded to salvage. If you like the shape and design, you can clean it with metal polish or even have it replated. Bear in mind that metal soap dishes can be spray-painted, but paint will not permanently adhere to porcelain.

LEFT: *Many flea markets display wooden mantels in their classic form: a wide crosspiece supported by narrow legs.* OPPOSITE: *With a little work, most such mantels can be transformed into sleek upholstered headboards for double beds. Look for examples in one piece, with interesting details such as center crests or medallions. Some vintage mantels can be found for as little as $200, so the finished headboard is a bargain when you consider the materials, details, and workmanship.*

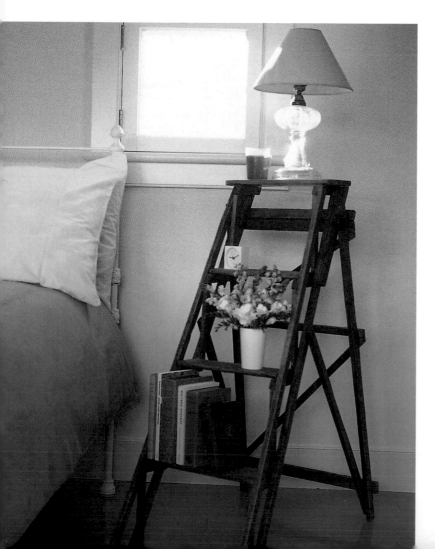

12.
MANTEL
headboard

MATERIALS *MANTEL, ¾-INCH PLYWOOD, FABRIC, COTTON BATTING, SANDPAPER, PAINTBRUSH, PRIMER, SEMIGLOSS PAINT, DRILL, STAPLE GUN, PINKING SHEARS, CONTRASTING FABRIC, DECORATIVE AND PLAIN BUTTONS, WIRE, WIRE CUTTERS, NEEDLE-NOSE PLIERS, WALL-MOUNT HARDWARE, NAILS, HAMMER, SCREWS.* 1. Cut plywood to fit inside negative space of mantel; cut fabric 6 inches larger than plywood all around and batting 4 inches larger than plywood. 2. Sand, prime, and paint mantel with semigloss. 3. On back of plywood, make Xs in an even pattern to indicate location of tufting. Drill small holes at those locations. 4. Lay batting on floor, center plywood on top, pull batting around edges, and staple to back. Repeat with fabric, covering plywood and batting. Fold edges under before stapling. 5. With pinking shears, cut circles of contrasting fabric 1 inch larger in diameter than your decorative buttons. For each tuft, bend 8 inches of wire into a U shape, thread it through both holes of button, punch wire through circle of contrasting fabric, and twist it into a single strand. From the front of the fabric-covered board, punch wire through one of the drilled holes in headboard, thread it through a plain button on the back, and knot the wire by pulling it tight, causing fabric to form a rosette. Repeat for each tuft. 6. Attach hardware for securing mantel to wall at tops of mantel legs, lay mantel facedown, and insert plywood. Fit should be tight. From the back, tack in ¾- to 1-inch finish nails at a 45-degree angle. 7. Install screws in wall, and hang headboard. Push bed against it.

13.
STEPLADDER
nightstand

MAKE EFFICIENT USE OF BEDROOM SPACE—ALWAYS AT A premium—by stacking bedside necessities on a shapely wooden stepladder. The wide rungs of this vintage model provide a steady perch for a row of books (no need for bookends), a bouquet of flowers, an alarm clock, a reading lamp, and a cup of tea.

MATERIALS *TIN BOXES, PROTECTIVE MASK, PAINT STRIP-PER, PAINTBRUSH, SINGLE-EDGE RAZOR BLADE, STEEL WOOL, SANDPAPER, POLISH, CLOTH.* ⚶ Wait until you have collected a number of tin boxes before you begin this project; it is more efficient than trying to recondition them one at a time. When using paint stripper, it's preferable to work outdoors. If you must be indoors, work in a well-ventilated area, wear a protective mask, and cover all work surfaces with newspaper. **1.** Remove paint from the boxes with paint stripper, following the manufacturer's instructions. **2.** Using a single-edge razor blade, peel the remaining paint from the boxes, taking care not to damage the underlying surfaces. **3.** With medium-grade steel wool, remove any rust spots and smooth away any pits in the metal. If scratches result, sand them with fine-grain sandpaper. **4.** Polish the boxes with a general metal polish or one formulated specifically for tin. Buff to a rich, mellow shine. Display a gleaming stack of boxes anywhere you could use some storage or a decorative element, but keep them away from moisture; tin rusts easily.

BELOW: *The tower of boxes on this desktop started out as mismatched painted tins. They were used at the turn of the century to package everything from typewriter ribbon to spices.* **LEFT**: *Because the paint is so often in poor condition, tin boxes can be found today at very reasonable prices. Collect several in various sizes, and get out the paint stripper. You'll have a charming desk display in no time.*

BELOW: *Seeking out the letters needed to adorn a coatrack is a good family activity. Don't try for uniformity: The initials should be as different from one another in style as the personalities they represent.* LEFT: *Using letters in various sizes and finishes adds to this coatrack's overall charm.*

15.

MONOGRAMMED
hooks

THEY MIGHT MAKE UP ONLY A SO-SO TURN AT SCRABBLE, BUT LETTERS THAT WERE once part of old signs are a clever way to identify a hook on the mudroom wall for every member of the family. With belongings neatly grouped, you'll no longer have to rummage under someone else's jacket to find your own buried scarf. It's fun to match the style of the letter to the personality of the owner. Is he steady, like the cast-brass *A* above? Smooth, like the enameled brass *O*? Or is he a little rough around the edges, like this hand-cut wooden *B*? Keep looking until you find the perfect letter for everyone. These vintage letters, acquired at a flea market at prices ranging from $2 to $30, are easy to install. Affix the initials above hooks with adhesive mounting squares, which can hold as much as two pounds, or use a heavy-duty two-part epoxy intended for most surfaces.

LEFT: *Old wooden doors often boast architectural details worth accentuating. If you happen upon a well-constructed beauty in a salvage yard but don't need another door, consider making it into a headboard.* **BELOW:** *A wooden cleat easily attaches the door headboard to the wall.* **BOTTOM:** *Painting the headboard in a color similar to your bedroom wall will give it a finished, built-in look.*

16.
DOOR
headboard

MATERIALS *DOOR, TABLE SAW, SANDPAPER, MITERED CROWN MOLDING, PAINTBRUSH, PRIMER, SEMIGLOSS PAINT, 1-BY-4-INCH BOARD, SCREWS, POWER SCREWDRIVER, WOOD GLUE, STRIP OF 1-INCH HARDWOOD, FINISH NAILS.*  When is a door not a door? When it's turned sideways and made into a headboard. Look for a solid-core door with horizontal panels—a common configuration. The rails (the ladderlike crosspieces that separate the door's panels) should form matching uprights at each end of the headboard, so you will probably need to trim one side to make them symmetrical. Measure your cuts to allow at least 1 extra inch at each end. Cut molding to fit width of headboard. **1.** Prepare trimmed door for painting by sanding, if necessary. Paint door and molding with primer, then with semigloss paint, using a contrasting color for the rails, if desired. **2.** To mount headboard, cut hardwood strip to a length that equals the headboard's width. **3.** Cut it in half lengthwise on a 45-degree angle. **4.** Secure one strip to the back of the door with wood screws and wood glue, and attach the second strip to the wall so the angles interlock to hang the headboard. **5.** To keep the headboard even on the wall, screw and glue a 1-inch-thick strip of hardwood, as long as the headboard is wide, to the bottom of the back of the door. **6.** Attach the molding with small finish nails. Touch up any holes with paint.

17.
DRAWER
shadow box

*IN AN INSPIRED UNION OF FORM AND FUNCTION, A SEC-*tioned drawer, opposite, can be hung on a wall and used to hold any small collection you would like to admire. A fresh coat of paint may be in order. This drawer was painted off-white, and each compartment was given a subtle shade of cool blue or green. Hang the shadow box securely to protect its fragile holdings.

BELOW: *Old louvered wooden shutters are one of the most common finds at salvage yards.* **RIGHT**: *Pick up three pairs of similar sizes (easy enough if the yard owners have just returned from a demolition site), and you have the makings of an airy cabinet evocative of the tropics or a summer house on Nantucket. Some simple tools, a little paint, and a weekend are all you need to complete this project.*

MATERIALS *LOUVERED WOODEN SHUTTERS, PAINTBRUSH, PRIMER, SEMIGLOSS PAINT, READY-MADE WOODEN LEGS, PLYWOOD, SAW, SCREWS, SCREWDRIVER, DRILL, WOODEN EDGE TAPE, SANDPAPER, HINGES.* ❧ Before you begin constructing the cabinet, remove existing hardware from shutters, and set aside one latch for doors. If hardware is broken or missing, buy a dead-bolt latch. Clean and prime the shutters, then paint with semigloss. Paint ready-made legs to match. Determine which shutters will be the sides, the front, and the back. Pairs used for front and back should be the same width; side panels should match. The length of all shutters should be the same. **1.** To make top and bottom, measure width and depth of the shutters as they will stand in finished cabinet. Cut two pieces of plywood to that measure. Screw ready-made legs into one piece for base. Measure the thickness of the left and right shutters and front and back shutters, and subtract from the width and depth of the plywood, respectively. Cut two smaller pieces of plywood to the new, smaller measure. Center one smaller piece on top of each larger piece; screw together at corners. Paint plywood to match shutters. **2, 3.** Stand side shutters on bottom platform so each snugly abuts smaller piece. Screw to bottom edge, using number 8 screws. (To avoid splitting wood, predrill screw holes through shutters before attaching to bottom platform.) **4.** Fit top onto sides; attach shutters as in previous step. **5.** Attach back shutters as in previous steps. **6.** Cut plywood shelves to a measure that is 1 inch shallower than interior of cabinet. Trim fronts with edge tape. Paint to match rest of cabinet. Install shelves by screwing side and back edges to shutters from exterior. **7.** The front shutters should be slightly narrower than the back ones so doors will close smoothly; sand or trim ⅛ inch from each shutter if necessary. Use two 3-inch hinges per shutter to attach the doors. **8.** Remove old paint from sliding dead-bolt latch; repaint. Screw two latch parts to center of front shutters below pull rings.

FLEA-MARKET FURNITURE IS A REMNANT OF DECADES OF ECONOMIC AND SOCIAL CHANGE. SOME OF IT FINDS ITS

way to the thrift sale through obsolescence—these days there isn't much call for commode chairs, fire screens, or gout stools. Other pieces are outmoded by unfashionable designs, colors, or materials. Still others are simply the wrong size for contemporary living spaces. These drawbacks—in the eyes of former owners—produce a multitude of opportunities for the flea-market forager. By looking past the original function of a bed or a chair and focusing instead on its fine wood, sleek contours, or eye-catching details, an alert shopper will discover a generous supply of inspiring raw material. Of course, little of the used furniture that shows up at tag sales and flea markets is in perfect condition, so keep your mind open to potential restoration projects. Although the United States customs service routinely classifies anything more than one hundred years old as antique, many antiques experts refuse to apply the term to most Amer-

ican pieces. This is because as early as 1840 much of the furniture made in this country was being produced in factories, rather than handmade by artisans. Such pieces are of little interest to most high-end furniture dealers, making them inexpensive fodder for those on the resale circuit.

Wood furniture abounds at the average flea market, but try to determine the composition of a particular piece before you buy. Is the wood soft or hard? Solid or veneer? The answer may help determine possible refurbishing options, including methods of stripping, staining, and painting.

TYPES OF WOODEN FURNITURE

Before deciding how to deal with a shabby piece of furniture, you need to determine whether it is solid wood or veneered—that is, constructed of inexpensive wood and then covered in thin strips of a finer wood. Examine a place where several sections of the piece converge. Tiny dark lines along such divisions will indicate that you probably have a veneered piece. It's also a good idea to look at the corners; if the piece is veneered, the grain will not be continuous. If you still can't tell, look at the wood grain. If the piece is solid wood, the grain will have a certain logic to it, while the grain on veneered pieces may run in several improbable directions.

Veneer is quite difficult to refinish. If it is in very good shape, you can try to remove the old varnish, working gingerly, with denatured alcohol and fine steel wool. Then apply a fresh coat of varnish. But if the veneer is chipped or scorched, your best bet is to paint the piece and hide its imperfections.

Solid wood offers more refinishing options than veneer, but first you will need to determine if the wood is hard or soft. Hardwoods, including mahogany, walnut, birch, sycamore, cherry, maple, and oak, generally have a tight grain and are quite heavy. Softer woods, such as common pines, poplar, and gumwood, exhibit a more open grain and are considerably lighter in weight. To determine the type, try this test: Press the wood with your fingernail. If the nail easily sinks into it, it is a softwood.

Both hardwoods and softwoods may be refinished with paint or stain, but with varying degrees of success. Softwoods absorb paint and stain well. Milk paint, one of many refinishing options, is a combination of milk, lime, and pigment that has a chalky, old-fashioned appearance, as if it has been absorbed into the grain. You might also choose a high-gloss or an oil-based paint.

Because hardwoods have a much more dense grain than softwoods, they do not absorb stain or paint as well or as quickly as softwoods do. Depending on the individual piece and its condition, you could use lacquer, varnish, linseed oil, or Butcher's Wax to refinish furniture constructed of hardwood.

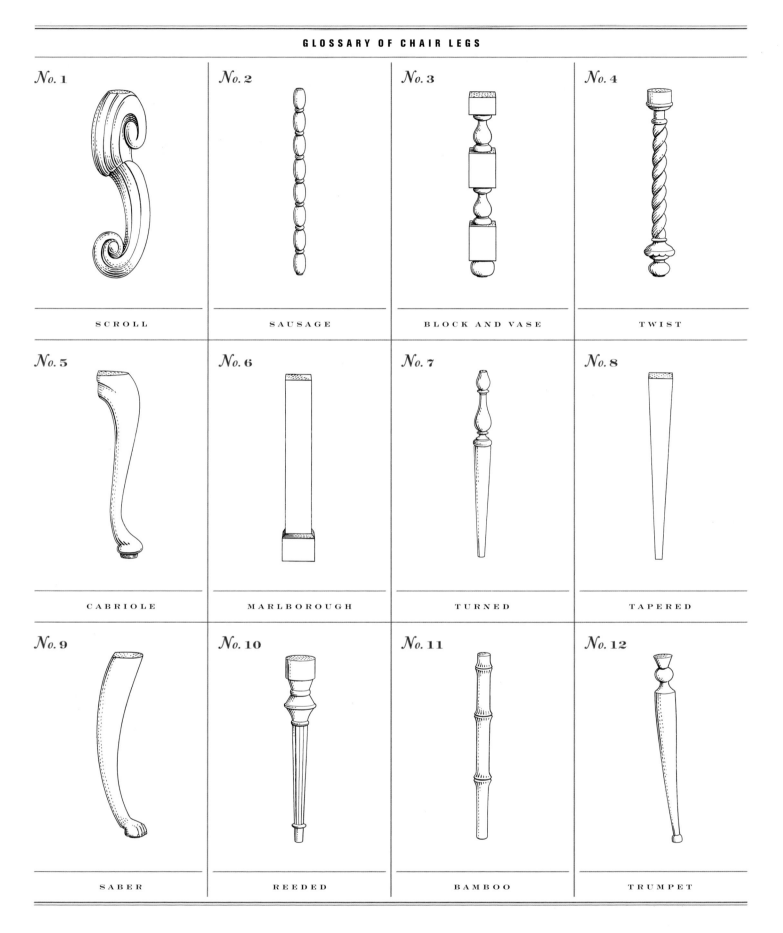

No. 1 — SCROLL

No. 2 — SAUSAGE

No. 3 — BLOCK AND VASE

No. 4 — TWIST

No. 5 — CABRIOLE

No. 6 — MARLBOROUGH

No. 7 — TURNED

No. 8 — TAPERED

No. 9 — SABER

No. 10 — REEDED

No. 11 — BAMBOO

No. 12 — TRUMPET

REPAIRING A LOOSE JOINT

The joint is the structural foundation of most wooden chairs. A strong joint can bear heavy loads; if it stays strong, the joint—and the chair—will remain stable for years. When a chair starts to wobble, one or more of its joints is probably loose.

1. A joint in this chair has separated and is ready to be reglued. A joint comprises two pieces, or members: One member, the tenon, protrudes from the end of a horizontal rail (the horizontal pieces joined to a leg at each end for stability); the other member, the mortise, is a cavity in the leg. The tenon should fit snugly into the mortise. **2.** To remove old glue, first clean the joint with a solution of one part vinegar to one part water, heated to just below boiling and applied with a metal spoon (wear rubber gloves to protect your hands from the hot liquid). This will soften the old glue, which you can then rub off the tenon and mortise with steel wool, being careful not to damage the wood. **3.** Apply new wood glue liberally to the tenon and mortise with a cotton swab, and insert the tenon into the mortise. Repeat steps 2 and 3 with other loose joints. **4.** Once all loose joints have been cleaned, reglued, and refitted, set the joints using pressure. First, loosely wrap string around all four legs, forming a rectangle. Repeat wrapping several times, leaving the string somewhat loose. If you are repairing the joints nearer the seat, wrap the string around the legs between the seat and the rails. **5.** Pull two ends of the string toward the middle until they just overlap. Cut the string, leaving an ample length of string at one end, then tie the two ends together. Insert a pencil between the overlapping lengths of string, and twist until the string feels taut. **6.** Place a tall object (we used a large Mason jar) in the middle of the legs to hold the pencil in place as the glue sets. Wipe excess glue from around the joints; let the glue set at least several hours. Remove the string.

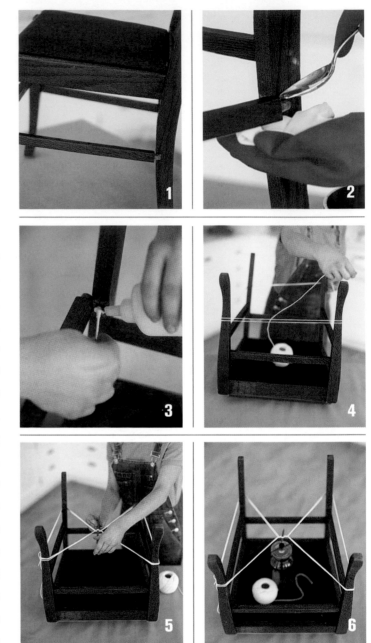

FINISHING OPTIONS FOR WOOD

A WAXED FINISH: This treatment replicates the look of aged milk paint. The buffed wax gives a sheen to the paint surface and acts as a sealant, preventing the flat finish from picking up dirt. First wash the piece thoroughly to remove wax, oil, dirt, and mildew. Use one-half cup of phosphate-free powdered cleaner dissolved in one gallon of hot water. If the piece has a painted finish, add a small amount of bleach. Wearing rubber gloves, gently scrub piece with a sponge or a natural-bristle brush. Rinse with clean hot water. (If you have used bleach, neutralize it by wiping with a solution of one cup of cider vinegar and one gallon of water.) Towel-dry, then let dry overnight. Fill any cracks with wood filler, and then sand. Sand the entire piece with medium-grade sandpaper, then wipe it clean with a damp rag. Apply one coat of latex primer with a synthetic-bristle brush. Let dry according to the product instructions. Paint the piece with two

coats of latex paint, letting dry between coats. When completely dry, rub a clear paste wax such as Butcher's lightly over the surface with a clean cotton rag or sponge. Wipe off excess, wait at least fifteen minutes, then buff lightly with a clean cloth until a satiny shine appears. For a gently worn look, selectively sand edges and hinges with medium-grade sandpaper or steel wool until original paint color or wood is revealed.

PREPARING WOOD FOR REFINISHING: Wash the piece to remove wax, oil, dirt, and mildew. If the piece has been painted, strip loose paint with a scraper or a commercial stripping product. (Paint made before 1978 may be lead-based: Safely dispose of all chips, and keep children away from your work area.) Metal scrapers work well on flat surfaces. For softwood, which is easy to damage with a sharp metal scraper, and for curves and grooves, a chemical stripper works best. You can scrape off the bulk of the paint and then finish the tough spots with a chemical stripper. Wear goggles, a respirator (available at hardware stores), and gloves, and work outside or in a well-ventilated space.

Scrub the surface with a nylon abrasive pad soaked in mineral spirits, then wipe dry. Scrub the wood again with a solution of one pint of warm water and one ounce of ammonia. Wipe clean, and let wood dry overnight. Fill any dents or gouges with wood filler. Once the filler is dry, lightly sand the piece with medium-grade sandpaper, then wipe it clean with a damp rag or tack cloth.

This battered early-twentieth-century bureau, a flea-market find, awaits a new life as a freshly enameled, milk-painted, or whitewashed showpiece.

ENAMEL PAINT: Enamel paint provides a durable finish well-suited to any furniture that gets heavy wear or is exposed to moisture. First clean, patch, and sand your piece, following the instructions above for preparing wood. Apply an alkyd primer, using a natural-bristle brush. Let the primer dry for at least twenty-four hours. Apply two to four coats of enamel paint, always waiting at least twenty-four hours between applications. For a higher shine, use semigloss or high-gloss paint.

STAINING: To stain unpainted wood, first sand your piece. Start with coarse sandpaper (80-grade, for example), and work your way to fine (220-grade), taking care to sand with the grain of the wood, not across the grain. It is important to sand evenly, using the same grade sandpaper on all parts of the furniture so that the stain will adhere evenly. Apply stain liberally with a brush, allow it to soak in, then wipe it off with a clean, lint-free cloth after five to fifteen minutes. For a darker stain, add a second coat.

WAXING: Wax wood furniture with a good clear paste wax such as Butcher's. Before waxing, clean thoroughly with a mild cleaner. If stains persist, try a mild solvent such as mineral spirits. Old wax spots can be removed with a product made specifically to remove wax from wood furniture; look for it at hardware stores. Fold a cotton rag or piece of cheesecloth into a square, then rub it in wax to coat. Liberally apply to wood, and wax a manageable area. Allow ten to twenty-five minutes for the wax to dry, then buff lightly with a clean cloth until a satiny shine appears. The timing is important. If you don't wait long enough, you'll simply wipe the wax off again, but if you wait too long, it will be too hard to buff. You may have to experiment on an inconspicuous part of your piece to determine the proper interval.

CLEANING FURNITURE MADE OF OTHER MATERIALS

Flea-market furniture comes in a variety of materials other than wood. You may encounter tables with Formica tops, or pieces made from rubber, linoleum, chrome-plated metal, fiberglass, an early plastic such as Bakelite, or Lucite (common in the 1960s and '70s). Cleaning methods vary by material:

✦ When cleaning any piece made of plastic, avoid ammonia in

Their paint may be peeling, or the metal may be rusted to the color of cayenne pepper, but with a bit of work, vintage pieces of garden furniture such as these chairs can be restored to their original attractive selves.

any form. Ammonia, the enemy of all plastics, will ruin its surface.

✦ Unfortunately, Formica and linoleum can be only superficially cleaned. If the damage is extensive, consider covering the entire piece with a latex or acrylic paint.

✦ To buff scratches on Lucite, invest in a heavy grade polishing cream, available at hardware stores. Avoid Lucite with chips and cracks, as these cannot be repaired or concealed.

✦ To clean fiberglass, use a nonabrasive cleanser. If furniture made of fiberglass is badly damaged, you can fill any cracks with a household sealant, then sand it and paint with latex paint.

✦ See pages 86 and 87 for tips on cleaning enamel and chrome.

RESTORING METAL GARDEN FURNITURE

STRIPPING PAINT AND REFINISHING: **1.** Metal outdoor furniture may be covered in layers of paint, leaving any decoration less crisp and once-sleek lines blurred. Before you embark on a refinishing job, make sure the piece is structurally sound. Examine it for weak spots or suspect welded joints. It is not worth the effort to try to refinish a piece in poor condition. **2.** Apply paint stripper in one direction with a clean, disposable paintbrush. Always work outdoors or in a well-ventilated area, wearing gloves and a respirator (available at hardware stores) to protect against fumes. **3.** When the paint loosens, remove it with a scraper, following the stripper manufacturer's instructions. You may need to use steel wool and/or a wire brush to remove remaining paint from any nooks and rounded edges (see photo 6). Paint made before 1978 may be lead-based: To be safe, keep children away from your work site and strip furniture over a drop cloth. Collect paint chips or debris on the cloth, and arrange for safe disposal with your local sanitation department. **4.** Wash the stripped piece thoroughly with water and a commercial product such as Spic 'n' Span to remove any paint dust or traces of stripper, and dry it immediately with a soft cloth. **5.** If you are not applying a chemical stripper, you can use a wire wheel attached to a drill. Use a handheld wire brush for small jobs, or attach a wire wheel to a drill for larger projects. Wear safety goggles in either case, and don't let the moving bristles linger too long in any area or you'll wear away the metal. **6.** Again, use steel wool in spots. Burnish scratch marks with fine steel wool or sandpaper (start with 320-grade and work your way up to 600-grade, if necessary). Wash piece again, and dry completely. **7.** Choose your finish. If you like the look of raw metal, seal surfaces with polyurethane, lacquer, or Val-Oil, a clear, hard-coat sealer. You can achieve the same effect with linseed oil or heated paste wax such as Johnson's, but you'll need to reapply it once a year. Paint is an easier option. Begin by spraying or painting furniture with a rust-inhibiting metal primer; such primers are usually red, white, or gray. Let dry. **8.** Apply a durable, oil-based outdoor paint.

1.

TABLE
sink stand

MATERIALS *TABLE, SAW, PORCELAIN BASIN, HIGH-GLOSS ENAMEL PAINT, PAINTBRUSH, SINK HARDWARE, COUNTERTOP MADE OF A SOLID SURFACING MATERIAL SUCH AS CORIAN, WATER-RESISTANT ADHESIVE (BASIN, TUB, AND TILE GLUE), TOWEL BAR (OPTIONAL).* You can use any table with an apron that is deep enough to hide a sink bowl. The countertop should have a ½-inch lip on the sides and front, and ask the store where you buy it to cut a hole in the countertop in which to place your basin (bring the basin along with you to ensure a good fit). **1.** Remove the old tabletop: You may have to unnail, unscrew, or unglue it, depending on its construction. **2.** If the table has cross supports, use a saw to remove the sections necessary to make room for the basin without compromising the table's stability. **3.** Paint all but the top of the table with high-gloss enamel, which will resist water. **4.** Once you have inserted the basin and its hardware into your countertop, squeeze a thick layer of the glue onto the top of the table, and carefully position the countertop. **5.** After glue is dry, have a professional connect the plumbing. **6.** Install an attractive towel bar at the center of the front, if desired.

ABOVE AND OPPOSITE: *The weak spot of many an otherwise attractive old kitchen table is a badly chipped or pitted top. A table with a good support structure may be an ideal candidate for transformation into a sink stand, which gives a bathroom a custom look and allows for valuable storage space underneath.*
RIGHT AND OPPOSITE: *Similarly, an old wooden coatrack can be spruced up with matching paint and easily transformed into a place to hang extra towels and robes.*

2.

COATRACK
towel holder

WOODEN COATRACKS WERE FOUND IN MANY HOUSEHOLDS in the days before front-hall closets. Now, these furniture staples are common finds for those who trawl flea markets and tag sales. Take one home, and use it in the bathroom—most bathrooms are forever in need of additional places to hang towels and bathrobes. For a quick makeover, clean the rack, then prime and paint its wooden parts with high-gloss enamel, which will repel moisture. We used white paint, chosen to match the sink stand, and polished the hooks with a product specially formulated for brass.

BELOW: *Benches such as this one were used to keep containers of preserved food off the cellar floor and were called crock tables. Many such functional pieces were never painted and, over the years, their unadorned surfaces have taken on a rich, pickled patina.* **RIGHT**: *If you happen upon one, take advantage of its weathered beauty by adding doors to it to create a cabinet.*

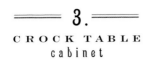
CROCK TABLE
cabinet

MATERIALS *FROSTED PLEXIGLAS, CROCK TABLE, WINDOW GLIDER TRACKING, 1-INCH SCREWS (OPTIONAL), POWER SCREWDRIVER, EYELET SCREWS, HEAVY-GAUGE BRAIDED WIRE, PLIERS, WIRE CUTTERS, LATEX PAINT, PAINTBRUSH.* Have two pieces of Plexiglas cut to fit cabinet, with a 1-inch round hole cut at the midpoint of one end of each front piece for the finger grip. Have tracking cut to fit at a hardware or building-supply store. If the cabinet requires a back, have another piece of Plexiglas cut to fit the outside perimeter, then have holes drilled every 6 inches all the way around. (You might also want to make holes for cords, should you wish to place any electronics inside the cabinet.) If using a back, attach Plexiglas through predrilled holes with 1-inch screws. **1.** Insert four eyelet screws in table "legs," below the lower shelf and equidistant from front and back, about 1 inch from top and bottom. (Screws should be ¼ inch shorter than thickness of legs.) **2.** Attach guy wires to help stabilize the cabinet: Starting at the bottom of one leg, send a length of wire through the eyelet, and twist it around itself to secure. Send other end of wire through the top eyelet on the opposite side of the piece, pull taut, and cut off excess. Repeat on other side of table. **3.** To enhance the pickled finish, dilute latex paint with water to desired level of opacity. Start with three parts water to one part paint; for more color, add paint. Brush it on table. **4.** For cabinet front, install the two tracks along top of bottom shelf and underside of top shelf. **5.** Slip the pieces of Plexiglas into the tracks, with finger holes at opposite ends.

4.

STEP STOOL
telephone stand

THE BROAD, STURDY STAIRS OF A VINTAGE METAL OR wooden step stool provide just the right amount of space for a telephone, notepad and pencils, city directory, and personal phone book. The portable station can free up your kitchen counter or create a small telephone center in a front hallway.

Because its top still folds down and up, our step stool–turned–telephone stand can—for lengthy conversations—become a chair. It also folds up for easy storage.

LEFT: *When vintage dressers are left outside or in a cold warehouse, they sometimes warp, making it difficult to slide the drawers in and out. The drawers themselves, however, may remain protected and thus in good shape.* **OPPOSITE**: *If you find such drawers, consider using them for under-bed storage. Leave perfectly good dressers for other shoppers; this project calls for one that has seen better days.*

5.

UNDER-BED
drawer storage

MATERIALS *DRAWERS, 1-INCH PLYWOOD, SAW, DRILL, FLUSH-MOUNTED WHEELS, WOOD GLUE, SCREWDRIVER, SEMIGLOSS PAINT, PAINTBRUSH.* ⚜ Look for drawers that will easily fit underneath your bed with at least 2 inches to spare for the wheels and the added plywood. **1.** Cut plywood to cover the bottom of each drawer, and drill holes of the appropriate diameter for flush-mounted wheels (available at hardware stores), 2 inches in from the sides of each corner of drawers (left). Affix plywood to the undersides of the drawer by squeezing a line of wood glue around the inside perimeter of the plywood and an X of glue in the center. **2.** Following the package instructions, install wheels. **3.** Using semigloss paint, paint the inside of the drawers an unexpected festive color (we chose bright yellow). Remove the drawer pulls and paint the outside of the drawers a different color that coordinates with the room, also using semigloss paint. Replace drawer pulls, or add new hardware.

6.

DOLL BED
cat bunk

MATERIALS *DOLL BED, 3- TO 4-INCH-THICK FOAM, SEWING SCISSORS, CATNIP SACHET, COTTON BATTING, PILLOW COVER OR FABRIC REMNANT, SAFETY PINS, SANDPAPER, SEMIGLOSS PAINT, PAINTBRUSH.* ⚜ Turn a vintage doll bed into an irresistible place for catnaps. We had our mattress made by an upholsterer, but you can use foam and any standard pillowcase or a remnant of fabric. Be sure to choose something that's washable and easy to care for. **1.** Cut foam to fill the doll bed. Using sewing scissors, cut a slit in one side of the foam to create a pocket large enough to hold the catnip sachet; insert sachet. **2.** Wrap foam in batting. Insert the batting-covered foam into a pillow cover, or wrap fabric around it, tucking it and pinning underneath to tightly fit your kitty mattress. **3.** Sand and paint the bed. Once dry, place cushion on bed.

BELOW: *The stoves of the 1920s and '30s were designed to look like pieces of furniture, and they often sat on elegant Queen Anne–style enamel cast-iron legs. When the body of a vintage stove is too far gone to save, merchants may detach its cabriole legs and sell them on their own. Gracefully shaped and made of good-quality material, a set is worth taking home.* **RIGHT**: *Spruced up with a fresh coat of automobile paint, this set of stove legs has been given a new function as the support for a sturdy but sweet bedside table.*

7.

STOVE LEG
nightstand

MATERIALS *STOVE LEGS, HARDWOOD CUT TO DESIRED SIZE FOR TABLETOP, SEMIGLOSS WOOD PAINT, PAINTBRUSH, SPRAY ENAMEL, DRILL, PHILLIPS-SCREW BIT, SCREWS, WASHERS, FELT PADS.* **1.** For a tabletop, choose wood of a thickness appropriate to the size of the stove legs. (We sandwiched three ¾-inch layers of plywood with wood glue, weighted them with a paint can overnight to dry, and sanded the edges.) Paint the wood with semigloss; let dry. Paint the legs with spray enamel; let dry. **2.** Position legs at corners of tabletop, setting them slightly and evenly in from the edge. With a pencil, mark placement of holes in legs. **3.** Drill holes for screws at the markings. **4.** Thread a screw through a washer, then sink the washer through the hole in the leg and into the hole in the wood. Repeat with remaining legs. Apply felt pads to bottoms of legs.

8.

HALF TABLE
console

MATERIALS *DAMAGED WOODEN DINING TABLE, SANDPAPER, ACRYLIC PRIMER, SEMIGLOSS PAINT, PAINTBRUSH, DRYWALL SCREWS, 2-BY-2-INCH PIECE OF HARDWOOD (THE LENGTH SHOULD EQUAL FLAT SIDE OF HALF TABLE), POWER SCREWDRIVER, WOOD FILLER.* After years of service in various dining rooms, many a table loses a leg, acquires too many scratches, and ends up at a flea market with a low price tag. If such a table was made in two parts with an extending mechanism to accommodate a leaf, one half of it can be transformed into an attractive console for a front hall. **1.** Unscrew and discard the extension mechanism from the bottom of the table. **2.** Sand, prime, and paint the table with semigloss paint, then let it dry. **3.** Using drywall screws, screw the hardwood piece to the wall at the height of the underside of the tabletop so that the edge of the table will rest on this support. **4.** Screw the top of the table to the wooden support. **5.** Fill the holes from the screws with wood filler, and touch up with semigloss paint.

ABOVE: *This old table may look down and out, but look again: Made of quality hardwood and with simple, attractive lines, it is too good to pass up. Instead of embarking on an expensive repair job, salvage the parts still in good condition—half the top and two graceful legs.* **LEFT**: *With a little work, a broken castoff can become a console table of just the right style and proportions to complete an elegant front hall.*

9.

PHARMACY AND DENTAL
display cabinets

THE METAL CABINETS IN EVERY NEIGHBORHOOD PHARMACY AND DENTAL OFFICE IN the early- to mid-twentieth century projected a comforting aura of cleanliness and authority. Today, their smooth surfaces, strong lines, and good proportions make them a natural choice for reuse at home—in the kitchen, dining room, bath, or wherever else storage space is at a premium. Either strip and paint the piece with the proper paint for metal or polish its natural surface until it glows. Glass hardware adds more shine and some subtle decoration; also appropriate are drawer pulls and cabinet knobs made of pewter, enameled porcelain, or brass.

OPPOSITE: *A child's room is filled with restored office furniture, including a General Fireproofing 1645F flat-top desk and a stackable bookcase (below), both painted a lively shade of green.* **RIGHT**: *Towels are stacked and protected from moisture in a glass-doored bathroom cabinet made from an office bookcase (below left).* **BOTTOM**: *This charming bedside table was originally a 1950s medical cabinet.*

=== 10. ===

OFFICE FURNITURE
at home

===

STEEL AND ALUMINUM FURNITURE WAS A MAINSTAY OF the American workplace in the 1930s and '40s. Today, fans of minimalist design are restoring such pieces for use in the home. If battleship gray doesn't suit your decor, consider repainting. First, have the piece professionally stripped. A furniture restorer or sandblaster may agree to remove the old finish. For a smooth, durable surface, choose wet- or powder-coat painting: Wet-coat painting, done at an auto-body shop, is expensive but offers more color choices. For powder-coat finish, fine, dry pigment is applied to an electrically charged object, then baked in a large oven; the process is less expensive, but color choices are limited, and painters willing to work on an individual piece may be hard to find. Try painters listed in the Yellow Pages, and be persistent.

OPPOSITE: *This coffee table was created by shortening the legs of a full-height table. Vintage coffee tables are hard to come by, but full-sized tables often make good conversions: Many have legs whose ends are worn from years of use, or rotting because they were stored in a damp basement or outdoors.*
BELOW: *A delicate wirework plant stand creates the atmosphere of a nineteenth-century conservatory— with or without plants.*

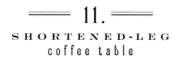

11.
SHORTENED-LEG
coffee table

UNTIL THE MID-TWENTIETH CENTURY, THERE WAS NO such thing as a long, low-slung table to place in front of a sofa where it could support a coffee cup or a pair of tired feet. Consequently, vintage coffee tables are in short supply, but you can create your own from one of the many full-height tables you come across. Simply cut down any well-shaped example, and, if necessary, replace the top with a piece of marble, slate, or galvanized steel. Measure your sofa to determine the desired table height, and saw the legs off evenly so the piece doesn't wobble. If the legs are carved or turned (as shown at left), cut them so that the remaining portion retains interesting contours.

12.
WIRE PLANT STAND
sideboard

WHEN THERE IS NO ROOM FOR A FULL-SIZED SIDEBOARD near a dining table, a vintage wire plant stand compactly handles the job. Although it might take up less floor space than a dining chair, its steady tiers provide plenty of room for dishes waiting to be served, sauces and condiments, or cutlery for the next course. When no guests are expected, a whimsical Gothic stand like the one at right creates a conservatory atmosphere and offers display space to anything you want to show off—a bowl of seashells, a collection of porcelain, or, naturally, a cluster of plants.

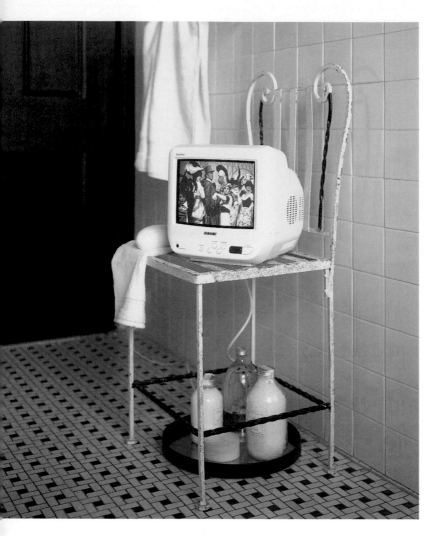

THIS PAGE AND OPPOSITE: *Vintage metal outdoor furniture, such as a garden chair (left) or a plant stand (opposite and below), are naturals for new uses in the bathroom. Built to withstand moisture, they evoke the light and fresh air of a garden and terrace.*

13.
GARDEN CHAIR
TV table

ANY STURDY CHAIR CAN ALSO FUNCTION AS A SMALL TABLE, as long as it has a flat, uncushioned seat. Look for lone survivors of sets—they are nearly always available at bargain prices. A white painted metal garden chair with a gracefully scrolled back makes a handy support for a small television. Because it was designed for outdoor use, its surface repels moisture, making it a fine choice for a bathroom stand. Instead of freshening up our find with a can of white spray paint, we decided to retain the slightly chipped look, which highlights its vintage charm.

14.
PLANT STAND
shelving

THE PETAL-FORM CUPS OF THIS ENAMELED CAST-IRON plant stand (opposite and left) are a convenient repository for the paraphernalia of comfortable bathing. An unusual triangular base and branching arms add a fanciful sculptural touch. Originally meant to hold flowerpots, such a stand features a weighted base, which will keep it firmly upright when fully loaded. Retain its patina, or enamel it in the color of your choice. Place a plant stand near the tub in your guest bathroom, and outfit it with bath-time essentials such as bath salts, oils, and a natural sponge. If towel racks are in short supply, pile extra linens on its arms.

Items pictured but not listed may not be available or are from private collections. Addresses and telephone numbers of sources may change prior to or following publication, as may availability of any item.

Introduction

PAGES 6–15 Special thanks to Beverly Vidler, Edward W. Vidler, Robert S. Vidler Jr., and Cole Menderson; Bygone China Match, 1225 West 34th North, Wichita, KS 67204; 316-838-6010; China Replacements, 2263 Williams Creek Road, High Ridge, MO 63049; 636-677-5577; and the Daguerreian Society, 3045 West Liberty Avenue, Suite 9, Pittsburgh, PA 15216; 412-343-5525. "Regent" *TEAPOT, CREAMER,* and *SUGAR SET* by Adams (back left), and "Cream on Cream" *COVERED VEGETABLE DISH* (back right) by Wedgwood from Pattern Finders; 800-216-2446. "Rhodora" *TEAPOT* by Lenox (center), and "Shelley Bridal Rose" (Rose Spray) *GRAVY BOAT* (front right) from Chinatown; 888-768-8282. *"ENGLISH CHIPPENDALE"* by Johnson Brothers (front left) from Replacements, Ltd.; 800-737-5223. "Celadon on Cream" *DEMI-TASSE* and *SAUCER* by Wedgwood from Chinatown; see above. *AN-TIQUES DEALERS:* Judd Caplovich, 56 Risely Road, Vernon, CT 06066; 860-872-7894; Matthew and Helen Robinson, Trifles, 70 Front Street, Bath, ME 04530; 207-443-5856 (if closed, call for an appointment); Ross Bros., 28 North Maple Street, Florence, MA 01062. For more information on the Scott Antique Market, call 404-361-2000. *RECOMMENDED*

READING: U.S. Flea Market Directory, by Albert LaFarge (St. Martin's Press). *TAG SALES:* For information on the 450-mile Highway 127 Corridor Sale, in Kentucky, Tennessee, and Alabama, contact Fentress County Chamber of Commerce in Jamestown, TN; 931-879-9948 or www.jamestowntn.org/worlds.htm.

Glass

PAGE 16 *FLY CATCHER, MUFFI-NEER,* and *JELLY JAR,* from L. Becker Flowers, 217 East 83rd Street, New York, NY 10028; 212-439-6001.

PAGE 20 *RECOMMENDED READING: Milk Glass,* E. McCamly Belknap (Crown Publishing Group, 1998); *The Milk Glass Book*, Frank Chiarenza (Schiffer Publishing, 1998); *Collector's Encyclopedia of Milk Glass*, Betty and Bill Newbound (Collector Books, 1995); *American and European Pressed Glass in the Corning Museum of Glass*, Jane Shadel Spillman (Corning Museum of Glass, 1981). *VINTAGE MILK GLASS,* available from the Tomato Factory, 2 Somerset Street, Hopewell, NJ 08525; 609-466-9833. *MODERN MILK-GLASS MANUFAC-TURERS AND DISTRIBUTORS:* Boyd's Crystal Art Glass, P.O. Box 127, Cambridge, OH 43725; 740-439-2077. Fenton Art Glass Company, 700 Elizabeth Street, Williamstown, WV 26187; 304-375-6122. L.E. Smith Glass Company, 1900 Liberty Street, Mount Pleasant, PA 15666; 724-547-3544. Summit Art Glass, 4171 Sandy Lake Road, Ravenna, OH 44266; 800-325-7547. Glass *KUGELS,* from Barbara Trujillo

Antiques, 2466 Main Street, P.O. Box 866, Bridgehampton, NY 11932; 631-537-3838.

PAGES 22–23 *CUSTOM FRAME,* from Chelsea Frames, 207 Eighth Avenue, New York, NY 10011; 212-807-8957.

PAGE 25 *PAPER LAMPSHADE,* from Just Shades, 21 Spring Street, New York, NY 10012; 212-966-2757.

PAGE 26 *GLASS-ETCHING KIT,* including 12-oz. bottle etching cream, camel-hair brush, and rub-on stencils, from Martha by Mail, 800-950-7130 or www.marthastewart.com. *ETCHING CREAM* (15-0150), from Etch-world; 800-872-3458 or www.etchworld.com. *DRINKING GLASSES,* from Takashimaya, 693 Fifth Avenue, New York, NY 10022; 212-350-0100 or 800-753-2038.

PAGES 30–31 Special thanks to Tony Ruffin of Aqua Art, 88 North 11th Street, Brooklyn, NY 11211; 718-302-9080. *WATER PLANTS,* available from Aquarium Driftwood; 800-600-4132; and from Aqua Art; see above. *AQUAT-IC PLANTS* and *LIGHTING,* from Arizona Aquatic Gardens, P.O. Box 91828, Tucson, AZ 85752; 520-742-3777 or www.azgardens.com.

PAGES 32–33 Special thanks to Scott D. Appell, 212-966-4745. *TERRARIUM PLANTS,* available from Logee's Greenhouses, 141 North Street, Danielson, CT 06239; 860-774-8038, 888-330-8038 or www.logees.com; Karutz Greenhouses, 1408 Sunset Drive, P.O. Box 790, Vista, CA 92083; 760-941-3613. *CARNI-VOROUS PLANTS,* from California

Carnivores, 2833 Old Gravenstein Hwy. South, Sebastopol, CA 95472; 707-824-0433 or www.californiacarnivores.com. *RECOMMENDED READING: The Savage Garden: Cultivating Carnivorous Plants,* Peter D'Amato (Ten Speed Press, 1998); *Successful Terrariums: A Step-by-Step Guide,* Ken Kayatta and Steven Schmidt (Houghton Mifflin, 1975; out of print); *Terrariums and Miniature Gardens* (Lane Magazine & Book Company, 1973; out of print); 9"-tall antique *FISHBOWL,* from L. Becker Flowers, 217 East 83rd Street, New York, NY 10028; 212-439-6001. Mexican river *STONES,* from Archetique Enterprises; 212-563-8003. Japanese river *ROCKS,* available from the Grass Roots Garden, 20 Jay Street, Brooklyn, NY 11201; 718-923-9069.

PAGE 34 Pure *HERBAL OILS,* from Aveda; 800-328-0849.

PAGE 37 *FRUIT JARS,* available from Leo Goudreau, 11 Richfield Avenue, Ware, MA 01082; 413-967-5054. *JARS WITH SCREW TOPS,* from Main Street Antique Center, 156 Main Street, Flemington, NJ 08822; 908-788-6767.

Fabric & Notions

PAGE 42 Special thanks to Beverly Vidler, Edward W. Vidler, Robert S. Vidler Jr., and Cole Menderson.
PAGE 43 Special thanks to Cheryl Anderson, weaver; Eric Jonson, gardener; and Lawrence Yerdon, president, Hancock Shaker Village, P.O. Box 927, Pittsfield, MA 01202; 413-443-0188. *ANTIQUE LINENS,* available from: Cobweb, 116 West Houston Street, New York, NY 10012;

212-505-1558. Kay Mertens, 1788 Everett Place, East Meadow, NY 11554; 516-538-9185. By appointment only. L. Becker Flowers, 217 East 83rd Street, New York, NY 10028; 212-439-6001. Legacy Antiques, 204 Sir Frances Drake Boulevard, San Anselmo, CA 94960; 415-457-7166. Main Street Antique Center, 156 Main Street, Flemington, NJ 08822; 908-788-6767. Paula Rubenstein, 65 Prince Street, New York, NY 10012; 212-966-8954. Trouvailles Française, 552 East 87th Street, New York, NY 10128; 212-737-6015. By appointment only. Vito Giallo, Town & Country, 352 Atlantic Avenue, Brooklyn, NY 11217; 718-875-7253. *RECOMMENDED READING: The Book of Fine Linen,* Françoise de Bonneville (Flammarion, 1994).

PAGES 44–49 Special thanks to C.J. Brown of Creative Visions, Staten Island, NY; 718-698-1697; Carol Wright of Wright Antiques, Delaware, NJ; 908-475-5513; Debra Bonito of Images Heirloom Linens and Lace, 32 North Colony Road, Wallingford, CT 06492; 203-265-7065; Linda Zukas of Linda Zukas Show Associates, P.O. Box 729, Cape Neddick, ME 03902; 207-439-2334 or www .vintagefashionandtextileshow.com (for information on the Antique Textile & Vintage Fashion Show in Sturbridge, MA); Sharon Stark of Sharon's Antiques; 610-756-6048 or www.rickrack.com; Carolyn Applegate; and Leslie Morava.
PAGE 45 *LAMP HARDWARE,* from Grand Brass Lamp Parts; 212-226-2567 or www.grandbrass.com. *VINTAGE FABRIC AND LINENS,* from Grand Remnants; 651-222-0221 or www.grandremnants.com.

Perennial *WOOL BLANKET* by Faribo, twin in bone white (0497), and *CASHMERE THROW,* in citron (0918), from Garnet Hill; 800-622-6216.

PAGE 49 Zig Zag embroidered percale *SHEET SETS* (0824), pure linen *BLANKET,* in flax (0490), and tailored cotton *BED SKIRT,* queen 14" drop (1406), from Garnet Hill; see above. Venetian Lace Hemstitch *LINENS,* Full Flat Sheet (SHS003), Standard Shams (SHS026), and Full Fitted Sheet (SHS004), from Martha by Mail; 800-950-7130 or www .marthastewart.com. Cream-and-gray felted merino cashmere *BLANKET,* from Greg Jordan New York; 212-570-4470.

PAGE 50 Umbra *CAFE HOOKS* in black, chrome, and aged brass, available from Gracious Home, 1217 Third Avenue, New York, NY 10021; 212-517-6300.

PAGES 50–51 *SWISS CLIPS* by JBC Imports and Marketing and ¾" pro-sheen silver *FOIL TAPE* by Pro Tape, both available from Pearl Paint, 308 Canal Street, New York, NY 10013; 800-221-6845 or 212-431-7932.

PAGE 53 Linen *TEA TOWELS,* from Dean & DeLuca, 560 Broadway, New York, NY 10012; 212-431-1691 or 800-221-7714. Stainless-steel ballpoint *CUP HOOKS* (DHTY2040) and nickel sew-on *RINGS* (RR7660422), from Gracious Home; see above.
PAGE 55 French Ivory *FLATWARE* (KFW008), from Martha by Mail; 800-950-7130 or www .marthastewart.com. *LAMP HARDWARE,* from Grand Brass Lamp Parts; see above.
PAGES 56–57 *PILLOW-CASING FABRIC* (used for both silverware

bag and to line suitcase), men's *SHIRTING FABRIC* (used for napkins), both at Beckenstein's Ladies Fabrics, 125 Orchard Street, New York, NY 10002; 212-475-7575. Rayon-blend *ELASTIC,* at M&J Trimming Co., 1008 Sixth Avenue, New York, NY 10018; 212-391-8731. *VINYL-COATED COTTON-BLEND FABRIC* (used to line silverware bag), at Fabric Place, 136 Howard Street, Framingham, MA 01701; 508-872-4888. *BOOKBINDER'S BOARD, GLUE,* and *BRUSH,* all from Talas, 568 Broadway, Suite 107, New York, NY 10012; 212-219-0770. Metal clamp-edge *FOOD TINS,* at Kam Kuo Food Corp., 7 Mott Street, New York, NY 10013; 212-349-3097.

PAGE 58 Self-healing *CUTTING MAT* (CTL001), from Martha by Mail; 800-950-7130 or www .marthastewart.com.

PAGE 60 Special thanks to Merlyn Colon, 212-967-4401; and to Kaethe Kliot of Lacis, 3163 Adeline Street, Berkeley, CA 94703, 510-843-7290 or www.lacis.com. *RECOMMENDED READING: Graced by Lace,* Debra Bonito (Schiffer Book for Collectors). *DOILIES,* available from Claire Walker, 48 Allen Street, East Longmeadow, MA 01028; 413-525-7178. *FRAMING SERVICES,* available from City Frame, 259 West 30th Street, New York, NY 10001; 212-967-4401.

Kitchenware & Ceramics

PAGE 64 Special thanks to Donald Wainland, custom metal fabricator of Wainlands; 212-243-7717; William Manfredi, master silversmith of William Manfredi, Silversmith; 212-260-5591;

Howard Newman, sculptor and restorer of art objects and statuary in metals and other materials in Newport, RI; 401-846-4784 or www.newmansltd.com; and Colin Stair, president of Stair Galleries & Restoration; 518-851-2544 or www.stairgalleries.com.

PAGE 65 Special thanks to Ernie and Bev Dieringer of the White Ironstone China Association; 203-938-3740 or www.whiteironstonechina.com.

PAGE 69 Special thanks to Rob and Olive Robinson of the Violet Barn, P.O. Box 9, Naples, NY 14512; 585-374-8592 or www.robsviolet.com. Catalog available. Also to Beall & Bell Antiques, 18 South Street, Greenport, NY 11944; 631-477-8239.

PAGE 70 Late-19th-century Scandinavian upholstered *PINE BENCH*, from Evergreen Antiques, 1249 Third Avenue, New York, NY 10021; 212-744-5664.

PAGE 71 18-gauge annealed *IRON WIRE*, from Metalliferous, 34 West 46th Street, 2nd floor, New York, NY 10036; 888-944-0909 or www.metalliferous.com.

PAGE 72 Large *TIN RINGS* (left, second from top, and center), *CONICAL RING* (right, second from top), *SCALLOPED MOLD* (bottom, center), *RIDGED RING* (bottom, right), and *TIN-PEAKED RING MOLD* (center shelf, front right), from Ryan's Antiques, 8 Burlington Road, Harwinton, CT 06791; 860-485-9600. 1840s French *SORBET MOLD* (top of pyramid), and pewter *ICE CREAM MOLD* (bottom shelf, back left), from Pat Guthman Antiques, 340 Pequot Avenue, P.O. Box 686, Southport, CT 06490; 203-259-7069. Large *TIN MOLD*, from Lisa

Worden through Sloane Square Antiques, 2 Somerset Street, Hopewell, NJ 08525; 800-598-8099. *RECTANGULAR TINS WITH DECORATIVE TOPS* (bottom shelf, fourth and fifth from back left), from Gore Dean Antiques, 1525-1529 Wisconsin Avenue, Washington, D.C. 20007; 202-625-1776.

PAGE 78 *EZ-GLIDE CIRCLES* (HEZ 001) in brown, 1 pack of 76 (contains 1" circles, ⅝" circles, and 1½" circles), from Martha by Mail; 800-950-7130 or www.marthastewart.com.

PAGE 79 18-gauge *COPPER WIRE*, from Metalliferous; see above. Nicopress *OVAL SLEEVES* from National Telephone Supply, 5100 Superior Avenue, Cleveland, OH 44103; 216-361-0221.

PAGE 81 *CERAMIC PLANTERS*, from the Tomato Factory, 2 Somerset Street, Hopewell, NJ 08525; 609-466-9833.

Hardware & Salvage

PAGE 84 Antique and reproduction *HARDWARE*, available from Crown City Hardware, 1047 North Allen Avenue, Pasadena, CA 91104; 626-794-1188.

PAGE 86 Circa-1860 French painted pine *TABLE*, from Rooms & Gardens, 7 Mercer Street, New York, NY 10012; 212-431-1297. *LINEN RUNNER*, from Paula Rubenstein, 65 Prince Street, New York, NY 10012; 212-966-8954.

PAGE 87 Vintage and antique *HARDWARE*, from Liz's Antique Hardware, 453 South La Brea, Los Angeles, CA 90036; 323-939-4403. Catalog available.

PAGES 90-91 Eastlake bin *PULLS*, available from Liz's Antique Hardware; see above. 19th-century

TABLE from Shanxi Province, from Sinotique, 19a Mott Street, New York, NY 10013; 212-587-2393. *RUG,* from Laura Fisher Antiques, 1050 Second Avenue, Gallery 84, New York, NY 10022; 212-838-2596. Similar *CAST-IRON URNS,* in scalloped (DCU002), iceberg (DCU003), and leaf (DCU001), from Martha by Mail; 800-950-7150 or www.marthastewart.com. *SHADES,* Onyx 848, Calypso Collection, available from Smith + Noble; 800-248-8888 or www.smithandnoble.com.

PAGES 92-93 Marble *MANTEL TOPS,* available from Moon River Chattel, 62 Grand Street, Brooklyn, New York 11211; 718-388-1121.

PAGE 95 Large *NESTING-RABBIT DISH,* in green glass (DGB002), from Martha by Mail; 800-950-7130 or www.marthastewart.com.

PAGE 96 Tiger maple *BOX,* custom sizes, available from We'll Make It for You Woodworking, Monessen, PA 15062.

PAGE 97 30"-by-18"-by-18" hinged *PLYWOOD BOX,* not painted, with blocks mounted inside, from Clover Woodworking, 1340 60th Street, Brooklyn, NY 11219; 718-854-6660. Drawing by Lloyd Goldsmith; www.lloydgoldsmith.com.

PAGE 98 *METAL TABLE,* from Guéridon, 359 Lafayette Street, New York, NY 10012; 212-677-7740. Martha Stewart Everyday Colors *PAINT* in Homespun (HO3) on wall, from Kmart; 800-866-0086 for store locations; also available from Sears mall stores; 800-972-4687 for locations.

PAGE 99 Custom *FRAMING,* from Chelsea Frames, 207 Eighth Avenue, New York, NY 10011; 212-807-8957.

PAGE 100 Garden *URNS,* from the Lively Set, 33 Bedford Street, New York, NY 10014; 212-807-8417; Treillage, 418 East 75th Street, New York, NY 10021; 212-535-2288. "Tapei" woolen *RUG,* available from Shyam Ahuja, 201 East 56th Street, New York, NY 10022; 212-644-5910.

PAGE 101 Lamp *HARDWARE,* available from Grand Brass Lamp Parts; 212-226-2567 or www.grandbrass.com.

PAGE 103 Custom-framed *MIRROR,* from Chelsea Frames, 207 Eighth Avenue, New York, NY 10011; 212-807-8957.

PAGE 104 Braun *ALARM CLOCK* (OWC001), from Martha by Mail; 800-950-7130 or www.marthastewart.com.

PAGE 105 Zig Zag embroidered percale *SHEET SETS* (0824), pure *LINEN BLANKET,* in flax (0490), and tailored cotton *BED SKIRT,* queen 14" drop (1406), from Garnet Hill; 800-870-3513. *HERRINGBONE FABRIC* and *FELT* for buttons on headboard, from B&J Fabrics; 212-354-8150. *BUTTONS* on headboard, from M&J Trimming; 212-391-9072.

PAGE 106 *PAINT* on wall (1388 flat) and on wainscoting (HC6), by Benjamin Moore; call 800-826-2623 for retailers.

PAGE 107 Five-panel *DOORS,* from Moon River Chattel; see above.

PAGE 108 *CEILING HOOKS* (580), from Simons Hardware, 421 Third Avenue, New York, NY 10016; 212-532-9220. Cashmere Donegal tweed *BLANKET,* from Greg Jordan New York; 212-570-4470. *LINEN SEWING BOXES* (CSW003), from Martha by Mail; 800-950-7130 or www.marthastewart.com.

Furniture

PAGE 112 Antique *CHAIRS,* available from the Olde White Church, 120 Oak Street, Hills, IA 52235; 319-679-2337.

PAGE 116–117 *RECOMMENDED READING: Furniture Restoration and Repair for Beginners,* Kevin Jan Bonner (Guild of Master Craftsman Publications, Ltd., 1995). *The Weekend Refinisher,* Bruce Johnson (Ballantine Books, 1989).

PAGES 118–119 *SAFETY HOTLINES:* Indoor Air Quality Information Clearinghouse, P.O. Box 37133, Washington, D.C. 20013-7133; 800-438-4318. U.S. Consumer Products Safety Commission, Washington, D.C. 20036; 800-638-2772. Sunburst-pattern *WROUGHT-IRON CHAIRS,* from Sage Street Antiques, P.O. Box 504, Sag Harbor, NY 11963; 631-725-4036. Bamboo-style *STEEL GARDEN CHAIR* with steel caned seat, from Urban Archaeology, 143 Franklin Street, New York, NY 10013; 212-431-4646 or www.urbanarchaeology.com. Hard-coat *SEALER,* by Val-Oil; call 800-845-9061 for nearest distributor. *PAINT STRIPPERS, RUST REFORMER,* and *NAVAL JELLY,* all from Gracious Home, 1220 Third Avenue, New York, NY 10022; 212-517-6300 or 800-338-7809. *PROFESSIONAL PAINT STRIPPERS* are listed in the Yellow Pages under "furniture stripping" (or "refinishing" or "sandblasting"), or contact local antiques dealers for referrals.

PAGE 121 "Holly's Center Set" *BATHROOM FIXTURE,* from Modern Plumbing Supply; 860-354-4448. Martha Stewart Everyday 5-Star Pima Cotton *BATH TOWELS,* in porcelain, from Kmart; 800-866-0086 or www.bluelight.com. White House *TOWELS* (LPT004), Industrial *END TABLE* (NRT002), and Ideal *ALARM CLOCK* (OWC001), all from Martha by Mail; 800-950-7130 or www.marthastewart.com.

PAGE 125 Venetian Lace Hemstitch *LINENS,* Full Flat *SHEET* (SHS003), Standard *SHAMS* (SHS026), and Queen Fitted Sheet (SHS005), from Martha by Mail; 800-950-7130 or www.marthastewart.com. Apple botanical *PRINT,* from Country Dreams Antiques and Collectibles; 888-262-1090. Rose *PRINT* by Ron van Dongan, at Peter Fetterman Gallery; 310-453-6463 or www.peterfetterman.com. Cream-and-gray felted merino cashmere *BLANKET,* from Greg Jordan New York; 212-570-4470.

PAGE 126 6'-by-9' striped Tibetan wool-and-silk *RUG* (721), from Odegard, 200 Lexington Avenue, 12th Floor, New York, NY 10016; 212-545-0069 or 800-670-8836. To the trade only. Martha Stewart Everyday Colors *PAINT* in Hooked Rug Green (D18) on nightstand, from Kmart; see above, and Sears, 800-972-4687.

PAGE 127 *PAINT* on wall, Homestead Green (AC-19 flat), and table, Elephant Gray (2109-50 semigloss), by Benjamin Moore; 888-672-4686.

PAGE 128 *DENTAL CABINET,* from Urban Archaeology; see above.

PAGE 129 Gilded *MIRROR;* sterling-silver *SPOONS* with *F* monogram by F.D. Brower & Son; late 19th-century American pressed *GOBLETS;* English Abbeyhorn *COMBS* and *BRUSHES;* and 1920s *DOCTOR'S CABINET;* all from Rural Residence, 316 Warren Street, Hudson, NY 12534; 518-822-1061 or www.ruralresidence.com.

PAGE 131 "Fawn, Trees, Blue Sky" hooked *RUG,* from Laura Fisher Antique Quilts & Americana, 1050 Second Avenue, New York, NY 10022; 212-838-2596. *CAST-IRON "JACKS,"* from Paula Rubenstein, 65 Prince Street, New York, NY, 10012; 212-966-8954. iMac *COMPUTER,* from Apple Computer; 800-538-9696 or www.apple.com. *PAINT* on desk and bookcase, Opel Bedford/Vauxhall (10) Linded Green; on fishbowl stand and stool, Saab/Acania (16) Brilliantgul; on cabinet, Saab/Scania (1) Marmorvit; all colors custom-mixed by Kalbacher's Auto, 33 Fort Pond Boulevard, East Hampton, NY 11937; 631-324-4244.

PAGE 132 *PITCHER* and *HIGHBALL GLASSES,* from Simon Pearce, 500 Park Avenue, New York, NY 10022; 212-421-8801.

PAGES 134–135 9" Sony *TV* (KV9PT60), from Sony Electronics, 800-222-7669 for locations. Milk *BATH SALTS,* all by Coté Bastide, and stainless-steel *TRAY,* from Ad Hoc, 410 West Broadway, New York, NY 10012; 212-982-7703. Antique garden *CHAIR,* from Paterae, 458 Broome Street, New York, NY 10013; 212-941-0880. *BATHTUB, EXPOSED BATH MIXER WALL MOUNT, SPONGE HOLDER,* and *SHOWER HEAD,* from Waterworks, 190 Main Street, Westport, CT 06880; 203-227-5008. *SOAP* by Savon, from Mottura; 415-872-8585 for nearest retailer. Antique marble *SHOWER BASEBOARD,* from Urban Archaeology, see above. Lead *TABLETOP,* from Sage Street Antiques, see above.

Index

STYLE EDITORS: FRITZ KARCH
AND BRIAN HARTER ANDRIOLA
TEXT BY ANN E. BERMAN

EDITORS: ELLEN MORRISSEY AND ALICE GORDON
ART DIRECTOR: BARBARA DE WILDE
DESIGN BY MARY JANE CALLISTER
ASSISTANT MANAGING EDITOR: SARA TUCKER
ASSISTANT EDITOR: CHRISTINE MOLLER
SENIOR DESIGN PRODUCTION ASSOCIATE: DUANE STAPP
DESIGN PRODUCTION ASSOCIATE: MATTHEW LANDFIELD
ASSISTANT ART DIRECTOR: JENNY HOITT

A SPECIAL THANK-YOU TO ALL WHO GENEROUSLY LENT THEIR time, talent, and energy to the creation of this book, among them Stephen Antonson, Eve Ashcraft, Roger Astudillo, Marc Bailes, Celia Barbour, Brian Baytosh, Douglas Brenner, Jesse Foley Brink, Claudia Bruno, Jane Burdon, Lee Alan Buttala, Dora Braschi Cardinale, Anthony Cochran, Peter Colen, Amy Conway, Jay Cooper, Nico De Swert, Cindy DiPrima, Tara Donne, James Dunlinson, Stephen Earle, Thomas Eberharter, Pat Fay and Carole Maddock of Those Two Girls, Jamie Fedida, Richard P. Fontaine, Stephanie Garcia, Amanda Genge, Melañio Gomez, Trish Hall, Eric Hutton, Elyse Kroll, Jodi Levine, Steve Levine, Sara Lorimer, Peter K. Mars, Laura Mathews, Jim McKeever, Hannah Milman, Pamela Morris, Laura Normandin, Elizabeth Parson, Eric A. Pike, George D. Planding, Debra Puchalla, Meera Rao, Tracey Reavis, Ben Rice, Margaret Roach, Rebecca Robertson, Paul Robinson, Ayesha Patel Rogers, Nikki Rooker, Scot Schy, Bill Shank, Kevin Sharkey, Colleen Shire, Susan Spungen, Lauren Podlach Stanich, Lindsey Taylor, Timothy Tilghman, Gael Towey, Alison Vanek, Laura Wallis, Lenore Welby, and Bunny Wong. Thanks also to Oxmoor House, Clarkson Potter, AGT. seven, and R.R. Donnelley and Sons. Finally, thank you, Martha, for inspiring us to celebrate the inherent beauty and creative possibilities of flea-market finds.